AMERICAN MARKETING ASSOCIATION

MARKETING

TOOLBOX

Identifying the Right Markets

David Parmerlee

AMERICAN MARKETING ASSOCIATION

MARKETING

TOOLBOX

Identifying the Right Markets

David Parmerlee

NTC Business Books
NTC/Contemporary Publishing Company

Library of Congress Cataloging-in-Publication Data

Parmerlee, David.
    AMA marketing toolbox. Identifying the right markets / David Parmerlee.
       p.   cm.
    Includes index.
    1. Marketing—Management—Data processing.   I. Title.
HF5415.13.P3247   1992
658.8'00285—dc20   92-14243
                                                      CIP

3 2280 00613 5941

Published in conjunction with the American Marketing Association
250 South Wacker Drive, Chicago, Illinois, 60606.

Published by NTC Business Books
An imprint of NTC/Contemporary Publishing Company
4255 West Touhy Avenue, Lincolnwood (Chicago), Illinois 60646-1975 U.S.A.
Copyright © 1993 by NTC/Contemporary
Printed in the United States of America
International Standard Book Number: 0-8442-3576-8
18   17   16   15   14   13   12   11   10   9   8   7   6   5   4   3

AMA Marketing Toolbox

Many marketing management books define marketing and provide terminology definitions. The *AMA Marketing Toolbox* has a different pur-pose. This series will guide you in collecting, analyzing, and articulating marketing data. Although there is some narrative that describes the components of marketing processes, these books define the relationships between the processes and explain how they all work together. The books also supply formats (or templates) to help you create sophisticated marketing documents from your data.

A SYSTEMATIC PROCESS . . .

Because markets change constantly and new marketing techniques appear all the time, a step-by-step system is needed to ensure accuracy. These books are process-based to allow you to be as thorough as possible in your marketing activities and document preparation.

. . . FOR PROFESSIONALS

Although these books are written with a "how-to" theme, they are written for marketers who have experience and who know marketing terminology and the objectives of the business function of marketing. The *AMA Marketing Toolbox* consists of the following books:

- *Identifying the Right Markets*
- *Selecting the Right Products and Services*
- *Evaluating Marketing Strengths and Weaknesses*
- *Developing Successful Marketing Strategies*
- *Preparing the Marketing Plan*

ROLE OF THE MARKET ANALYSIS

How does the market analysis you will perform in these books fit in with other market planning processes? The market analysis tells a story about a market and explains what, why, how, when, and where events and activities will happen. The analysis tells you whether entry into a particular marketplace is possible, what it will cost, and is the basis from which to develop marketing strategies that will allow you to compete. A market analysis can be tailored to any size company with any product or service.

The books in the *AMA Marketing Toolbox* series will help you go from data collection, to analysis, to planning and control, and eventually to implementation of marketing plans. The diagram below indicates where the books fit into this process.

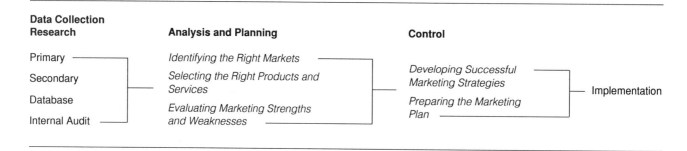

Data Collection
Research

Primary

Secondary

Database

Internal Audit

Analysis and Planning

Identifying the Right Markets

Selecting the Right Products and Services

Evaluating Marketing Strengths and Weaknesses

Control

Developing Successful Marketing Strategies

Preparing the Marketing Plan

Implementation

*This book is dedicated to every young child
with learning disabilities.*

Contents

Part 2 / Data Reporting: Formats 55

Introduction

WHAT IS A MARKET ANALYSIS?

A market analysis is an attempt at defining, identifying, and then evaluating the structure of a particular environment in which business activities happen—the marketplace. Its function is to apply research data and information that have been collected and tabulated, and place them in a document organized to give a detailed, accurate, and unbiased meaning. A market analysis should be performed every three to five years. If your market experiences great change every year (e.g., a high-tech market), an annual market analysis may be needed.

The market analysis gives you a clear understanding of marketplace dynamics in a set format. A thorough market analysis will give you an accurate picture of market size and trends. It will identify and profile your target audiences. It will show how your customers and prospects buy and what motivates them to buy. Most importantly, the market analysis provides direction so that you can qualify your markets and assess future market potential.

WHY PERFORM A MARKET ANALYSIS?

The purpose of performing a market analysis is to find out what to expect from the marketplace you are currently in or are considering entering. The market analysis will tell you how the market is constructed. It will tell you of any barriers or limitations to entering or expanding into the market, so you can determine what it will cost you to exist or compete. It will also tell you what the return will be; in other words, what the market is worth to you (market value) or what you can expect in terms of revenue generation (sales volume/earning potential). The market analysis is also the base from which you will develop strategies to achieve these returns.

By performing a market analysis, you are building the foundation of future marketing decisions. The golden rule in performing the market analysis is that you must be objective and read the market *as it actually is*. This means the analysis must not be structured around your product, service, or business. Though these may be mentioned as reference points, you must not make them central to the analysis. To do so could result in conclusions slanted toward your business, giving you an inaccurate picture of the market and defeating the purpose of the exercise. The analysis is based on market research activities and must be completely independent from research on the performance of your product, service, or business.

HOW DOES THE MARKET ANALYSIS RELATE TO OTHER MARKETING PLANNING PROCESSES?

The market analysis is the first section in a strategic marketing plan. The market analysis addresses only the market, not a company's product line in that market. If you are established and desire a product and service profile, it is suggested that you perform a marketing audit at the same time you perform the market analysis. If yours is a new business, a marketing audit would not be appropriate; a business plan would be a possible alternative. A business plan contains three basic marketing segments: a marketing plan, a product and service profile, and a market analysis.

WHAT IF YOU ARE PREPARING A SEPARATE MARKET ANALYSIS?

The marketing analysis, as stated earlier, is usually part of an overall marketing plan. However, if you are preparing a market analysis as an independent document, it should include the following elements:

1. Title page or cover page

2. Table of contents

3. Executive summary (including the purpose of the analysis and its major findings)

4. Methodology

5. Limitations

6. Market analysis (body of report)

7. Exhibits

HOW SHOULD THIS BOOK BE USED?

This book provides you with a set of 46 market analysis formats to help you prepare a document in which marketing research data can be presented in an organized fashion. Part 1 (Data Analysis) explains and demonstrates the use of the formats; Part 2 (Data Reporting: Formats) includes the blank formats themselves.

Before selecting and completing the formats, you will need to complete several other processes. First, you will establish objectives by answering such questions as: Who are our customers? Where is our market? How does it operate and perform? When do product purchases occur? Which certain external events affect our market? Second, you will set a budget, including cost allocation and a specific timetable. Third, you will design your market research strategy, including type of data collection, type of research, and project planning and design. Fourth, you will collect and process data based on your research strategy. Fifth, you will tabulate the data, perform statistical analyses, and generate reports. Sixth, you will analyze and evaluate your data and compare it with existing market research studies. Only after completing these six steps will you be ready to begin the processes of data processing and creating the market analysis document as explained in this book.

Throughout this book, you will be alerted to many possible adjustments you may need to make in the market analysis. To conserve space, each format shows a limited number of lines for products, whereas your firm may have fewer or many more products to consider. Another example of possible adjustments to be made is the format calling for sales of a product for the past three years. If your product is new, you will have no sales to date, making the current market share analysis impossible.

The processes and formats in this book are designed for a consumer market, such as consumer packaged goods or retail service outlets. Firms in special markets, such as not-for-profit organizations or institutions, can adapt the market analysis to their own market's needs, problems, and opportunities.

Part 1

Data Analysis

The five units in this book are designed to lead you through a step-by-step process of organizing data about your company, your product or service, and your market in order to create a market analysis document. Before using the formats in this book, you will need to have collected, processed, and tabulated data relevant to your particular marketplace. The formats in the book will help you use that data to create a clear, understandable document to direct and shape your marketing efforts.

Each unit defines factors that affect a market. When needed, the formats evaluate the past three years and the next three years in order to assess trends. The goal is to give you insight on how the market in question has evolved and where it is headed. By following the step-by-step process in these five units, you will have a clear picture of your markets, your customers, your competition, government regulations affecting your industry, and any existing market studies—all substantiated with hard data in a document that will give you confidence as a marketing decision maker.

Before you begin your research, read through this book to see what will make the analysis work and how to design your data collection methods to obtain the necessary information.

Unit 1

Identifying Your Markets

DEFINING YOUR MARKETS

Defining your markets is a process of putting a face on the market as it exists today. Markets can be defined in mass or divided into segments. Limiting yourself to selected market segments to gain more control in those segments is usually most effective. Establishing market segmentation begins with marketing research. Before you can segment your market, you must understand customer preferences, motivations, purchase intentions, and usage patterns to establish linkages and verify the market profiles you select.

Exhibit 1–1 illustrates the steps in selecting variables to define your market. In the consumer market, you will use geographic, demographic/socioeconomic, product usage, lifestyle and psychographic, shopping

EXHIBIT 1–1
Market Identification Model

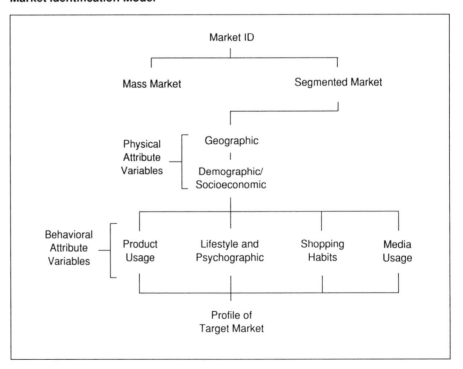

EXHIBIT 1–2
Market I.D. Process

1. Select market use patterns.

    a. Mass (If selected, skip to "Market Size," page 17.)

    b. Segmented

2. Identify segment markets.

    a. Select variables.

    b. Establish profile segments.

3. Define target markets.

    a. Evaluate profile segments' attractiveness.

    b. Select/prioritize profile segments.

habits, and media usage variables. You can select type or combine several types of variables to form your market segment profiles. (See Exhibit 1–2.)

Once you have selected your markets, give titles or IDs, for example, "The U.S. Home Consumer Electronics Market".

Market Segmentation and Your Target Markets

Identifying your market segments is called *target marketing*. The secret is to find a market where you can be a dominant player or at least a major player. To do this, you must establish criteria to effectively penetrate and compete in those target markets. The segmentation profile is made up of one or more physical or behavioral variables, which must be prioritized. These variables include geographic, demographic/socioeconomic, product usage, lifestyle and psychographic, shopping habits, and media usage attributes.

You may need to go through the market segmentation process several times to determine which market definition may work the best for you. The key to the whole process is the geographic location(s) of your market. As discussed, you must perform market research before you begin the entire market analysis process. That research will help you identify, define, and analyze potential customers for your product and/or similar products in the selected market. The objective is to take that research data and match it with variables in the segmentation process in order to see which geographic area has the highest number of potential customers.

Geographic Variables. You will almost always need to set physical boundaries for your market. This is done by selecting one geographic level or combining several, depending on your particular market. Geographic variables should be determined separately for each product line or individual product, if necessary.

To complete the following table, you must first select the level of the geographic area you choose to study. To give that level an identity, you'll need to call it by name (i.e. Census Tract 7301.03). You should identify not only the level you select, but several levels above it. This will give you a better point of reference and help you select the area(s) with which you wish to compare your target market. You will need to perform this analysis for each product/product line you are considering.

This table is based on the geographic levels established by the U.S. Bureau of the Census. Many research and database sources recognize these geographic levels as well as other "media-based" geographic levels. You may want to include these media-based levels as sub-geographic levels so that when examining existing research data you will have an equivalent basis of measurement.

Demographic/Socioeconomic Variables. The following six models give examples of possible items to use in performing market segmentation analysis. You will need to complete this analysis for each product/product line you are considering.

Format 1

Geographic Variables in Market Segmentation

Levels (Standard Unit)	Defined Area	
	Selection	Represents
Global/International	_____	_____
National	_____	*U.S.*
Regional	_____	_____
Divisional	_____	_____
State	_____	*Illinois*
County	_____	*Cook*
Minor Civil Division/ Census County Division (e.g., townships)	_____	_____
Places (city and town)	_____	*Chicago*
Census Tract/Block Numbering Area (population)	*X*	*7301.03*
Block Group	_____	_____
Block	_____	_____
Street	_____	_____
Place of Residence/ Place of Business	_____	_____

* Geographic Levels descriptors are based on the standards established by the U.S. Bureau of the Census, 1990 survey.

After you have decided the physical area of your markets, you need to profile the possible customers in those areas. This is done by inserting the demographic/socioeconomic data for those areas. In other words, you need to begin dropping in the numbers of human elements that exist in those areas. The first two variables used to convert the geographic numbers into population numbers are demographics (the who) and socioeconomics (the what). These two variables are based on U.S. Census counts of actual people and households, rather than samples based on statistical extractions of these people and households, which may not accurately reflect the actual people and households in those areas. Census-based data is a more reliable indicator of the basic structure of the population occupying the area you are evaluating.

To complete the following form, select the overall area or universe you wish to compare with the area you want to define. Remember, this is just an example—you may want to include other headings in your format such as degree of penetration (%). Drop in the numbers you have obtained from various sources in the columns for units, percentage, and index (which compares the two defined areas).

Index represents a formula that gives you a benchmark to determine how the two areas rank and/or rate. Interpretation may be different from vendor to vendor, and your understanding may differ from the source that prepared the data. However, it is generally recognized that indexing in this environment is performed using the following formula.

Using the demographic/socioeconomic variables:

Sex:

    male

Overall area percentage	42.67
divided by	40.28

Defined area
    multiplied by   x 100

$$\frac{42.67}{40.28} = 1.06 \times 100 = 106$$

The number 100 provides you with a baseline for comparison. If your defined market has scores above 100, it has a *higher* propensity to accept your product. If your market scores below 100, it has a *lower* than average propensity to accept your product.

Format 2

Demographic/Socioeconomic Variables in Market Segmentation

Overall Area (Universe): *State/Illinois*

Defined Area (Target): *Census Tract/7301.03*

Descriptor	Defined Area Units	%	Overall Area Units	%	Index (%)
Sex:					
Male	*3108*	*40.28*	*4703110*	*42.67*	*106.00*
Female	*4637*	*59.72*	*6320197*	*57.33*	*96.00*
	7745	*100.00*	*11023307*	*100.00*	

Age distribution:

2 – 5

6 – 11

12 – 15

(14 – 17)*

16 – 19

20 – 24

(18 – 24)*

25 – 34

35 – 44

45 – 49

(45 – 54)*

50 – 54

55 – 64

65 – 74

75 or older

* Note: variations in age breakdowns due to vendor variations.

Marital status:

Married

Widowed

Divorced or separated

Single (never married)

Parent

Living together

Education (last grade attended):

Grade school or less (grades 1–8)

Some high school

Format 2 (Cont'd)

Graduated high school

Some college (at least 1 year)

Graduated college

Graduate study

Full-time student

Part-time student

Occupation:

Armed forces

Employed

Full time
(More than 35 hours/week)

Part time
(Less than 35 hours/week)

Hold more than one job

Self-employed

Unemployed (looking for work)

Occupation

Managerial

Professional

Technical

Administrative support

Sales

Operative/Non-farm laborers

Service workers

Private household workers

Farmers

Craftsmen

Other

Not employed

Student (full time)

Homemaker
(not employed outside home)

Disabled temporarily

Retired

Ethnic classification:

White

Black

Hispanic

Asian

Format 2 (Cont'd)

American Indian

Other

Annual household income:

Under $10,000

    $10,000 – 14,999

    15,000 – 19,999

    20,000 – 24,999

    25,000 – 29,999

    30,000 – 39,999

    40,000 – 49,999

    50,000 – 74,999

    75,000 – 99,999

100,000+

Household producers:

Full-time earner

Part-time earner

Dual earners

Size of household:

(Age 18 or younger):

None

One

Two

Three or more

(Over age 18):

None

One

Two

Three or more

Householder status:

Rent

Own

Live with parents

Type of housing unit:

House

Apartment

Format 2 (Cont'd)

   Condo/townhouse

   Mobile home

   Other

Lived in area:

   Less than 1 year

   1 – 2 years

   3 – 4 years

   5 – 10 years

   11 or more years

Total

Product Usage Variables. After the physical area and the demographic data counts have been determined, you will establish the customer's behavioral attributes. Here you profile the various uses for a product/service and determine the various levels of purchasing activity, the factors that influence purchases, and the best methods of reaching those individuals regarding those purchase decisions. To do this, you will select one or more product usage variables.

Format 3

Product Usage Variables in Market Segmentation

Product Comparison Type: *Brand X*

Overall Area (Universe): *State/Illinois*

Defined Area (Target): *Census Tract/7301.03*

Descriptor	Defined Area		Overall Area		
	Units	%	Units	%	Index (%)
Heavy:	1002	12.94	3,034,872	27.53	213
Medium:	3020	38.99	5,866,101	53.22	136
Light:	3723	48.07	2,122,334	19.95	42
Total	7745	100.00	11,023,307	100.00	

In the consumer market, many products (yours and your competitors') offer similar features and benefits to a similar market type. The objective here is to evaluate a product with similar features to yours to determine how successful your product might be in that same market. Your goal is to measure consumption of similar products and rate them based on volume. You will need to perform this analysis separately for each product line or individual product under consideration.

For example, if you sell toothpaste, you will want to compare your product with another that is similar in characteristics such as name, packaging (pump or tube), form (gel, paste, or powder), and flavor (mint or regular).

Lifestyle and Psychographic Variables. Another method of defining your market is through the use of lifestyle and/or psychographic variables. This method identifies and measures personal traits and behavior patterns. This information can aid you in forming possible profiles of customers. When using the psychographic technique, it is important to understand its limitations. It is very effective in defining markets for big-ticket items, such as luxury automobiles; it is not very effective in markets for low-cost items. When using psychographics in profile analysis, keep in mind that it should only be used in conjunction with other variables, and not as a single source for decision making. You will need to perform this analysis for each product/product line you are considering.

Format 4

Lifestyle Variables in Market Segmentation

Overall Area (Universe): *State/Illinois*

Defined Area (Target): *Census Tract/7301.03*

Descriptor	Defined Area Units	%	Overall Area Units	%	Index (%)
Restaurant preferences:					
Fast food	3034	39.17	5,321,893	48.28	123.00
Full-service dining	2332	30.11	4,389,100	39.82	132.00
Fine dining	2379	30.72	1,312,314	11.90	39.00
	7745	100.00	11,023,307	100.00	
Leisure-time activities:					
Airline travel					
Sports participation					
Live entertainment					
Attend movies					

Format 4 (Cont'd)

    Rent videos

    Cable TV

    Home electronics

Health care usage:

    Hospital preference

    Clinic preference

    Insured

    HMO coverage

Banking/financial affairs:

    Investments (i.e., stocks)

    Debt financing

    Credit cards

    Debit cards

Auto ownership:

    Lease

    Own

    Bought new

    Bought used

    Foreign

    Domestic

Total

Format 5

Psychographic Variables in Market Segmentation

Overall Area (Universe): *State/Illinois*

Defined Area (Target): *Census Tract/7301.03*

Descriptor (Group ID)	Defined Area		Overall Area		Index (%)
	Units	%	Units	%	
Upper crust	34	0.44	17,008	0.15	34.00
Lap of luxury	12	0.15	28,021	0.25	167.00
Established wealth	14	0.18	11,073	0.11	61.00
Total	60	.77	57,102	.51	

Shopping Habits Variables. Another method in defining your market is through measuring shopping habits and activities by customer, by product line, and by place of purchase. This enables you to identify where purchases occur in relationship to the shopper's workplace and home. The objective here is to identify where customers shop and what influences their decisions to purchase. This information is very important when you get to the customer profile units where you will link customers by where they shop and where they live and work. This is called *store-specific analysis.* You will need to perform this analysis for every product/product line you are considering.

Format 6

Shopping Habits Variables in Market Segmentation

Overall Area (Universe): *State/Illinois*

Defined Area (Target): *Census Tract/7301.03*

Descriptor	Defined Area		Overall Area		Index (%)
	Units	%	Units	%	
Retail store preference:					
Department store	1045	13.49	2,023,755	18.36	136.00
Specialty store	2334	30.14	5,658,898	51.34	170.00
Supermarket	1298	16.76	1,000,230	9.07	54.00
Convenience store	2674	39.61	2,340,424	21.23	54.00
	7745	100.00	11,023,307	100.00	

Format 6 (Cont'd)

Shopping Motivation:

Price

Selection

Service

Quality

Location of store

Purchase patterns:

Store

Catalog/direct mail

TV shopping

Cash/check

Credit card

Coupon

Brand label

Major purchase intentions:

Car/truck

Computer

Furniture

Appliances

Home

Leisure

College education

Electronics

Total

Media Usage Variables. Another useful measure is the types of media customers may use when discovering a product and forming a desire to buy it. The objective with this variable is to establish what type of medium is used and when it is used. If you are assessing the impact of television on behavior, you may wish to determine program viewing habits for even more detail. You will need to perform this analysis for each product/ product line you are considering. Once again, depending on the vendor, some sources will combine these media activities and give you multiple usage data while others will total each item and provide single source usage data to determine the media usage level.

Format 7

Media Usage Variables (by Medium Used)

Overall Area (Universe): *State/Illinois*

Defined Area (Target): *Census Tract/7301.03*

Descriptor	Defined Area		Overall Area		Index (%)
	Units	%	Units	%	
Direct:					
Mail	803	10.37	1,256,450	11.40	110.00
Phone	75	0.37	999,767	9.07	935.00
Outdoor:					
Billboard	345	4.45	2,311,189	20.97	471.00
Transit	176	2.27	1,998,900	18.13	799.00
Television:					
Cable	1198	15.47	4,783,991	43.40	281.00
Broadcast					
Radio:					
Spot					
Print:					
Newspaper					
Magazine					
Insert (FSI)					
Special:					
Yellow Pages					
Total	7745	100.00	11,023,307	100.00	

In addition, you will need to be aware if your data is indicating time usage. For example, does your data define the media used by daytime versus nighttime, or week days versus weekends?

Establishing Criteria for Formulating Your Target Markets

After you have compiled the market characteristics in the preceding formats, you will need to organize your selected market configurations. This is done by taking the various market combinations and selecting one or several target markets to pursue. First, break down your market data into several groups, or target markets. This is done by selecting and establishing criteria made up of the market segmentation variables and their corresponding counts. Depending on the product, each profile will contain as many different variables as necessary. For example, if you are marketing toilet paper your variables will be product usage, demographics/socioeconomics with selected descriptors. On the other hand, if your product is a luxury automobile, lifestyle and psychographic variables will be included. The result is a defined market profile, such as the following:

Group 1	Counts
a. Ages: 45–49	2,678
b. Annual household income: $30,000–39,000	1,709

Full-court
"Mass marketing"

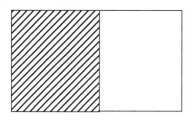

Half-court
"Segmented marketing"

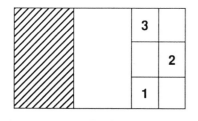

Selected spots
"Target markets"

Once this process is completed, you will assess each defined market profile's attractiveness. Once again, citing your market segmentation descriptors, you will rank each target market in order of importance. Placing these preferred segments into this structure will signal which markets you will be entering first. This is done by designating each segment as primary, secondary, or tertiary. The top markets are primary, the borderline markets are secondary, and the undesirable markets are tertiary. Now that you have completed your target market definition, you need to establish your niche definition—a narrative summary that establishes your mission and direction.

When segmenting a market, you are dividing your area into smaller, more manageable areas. Target marketing is the process of selecting and identifying the market(s) you will be viewing and, ultimately, in which you will market your products.

To understand the differences between a segment and a target market, review the examples shown at left.

If you have selected a mass market definition, the following sections will not have the same importance as if you had selected a segmented market. Nonetheless, you should take the following steps in determining your target market management.

Format 8

Target Market Formulation

		Target Market				
1			**2**			**3**
Descriptors	**Counts**		**Descriptors**	**Counts**		
Males	2,648,594		Males	9,846,575		
Age 20–24	4,446,509		Age 45–49	3,657,300		
White	2,367,444		Hispanic	5,674,974		
Total	345,346			234,562		

Totals represent cross-tabbed totals among descriptors, not total counts of descriptors.

Format 9

Evaluating the Attractiveness of Each Profile Segment

		Target Market				
1			**2**			**3**
Qualify						
Descriptors	**Counts**		**Descriptors**	**Counts**		
Males			Males			
Age 20–24			Age 45–49			
White			Hispanic			
Total	345,346			234,562		

		Target Market				
3 (#1)			**2 (#2)**			**1 (#3)**
Prioritize						
Descriptors	**Counts**		**Descriptors**	**Counts**		
Males			Males			
Age 45–49			Age 45–49			
White			Hispanic			
Total	234,562			147,654		

DETERMINING MARKET SIZE

Each identified target market must be defined by its size in a quantified format. The market size is divided into two levels or variables. The first variable is called the *market potential;* its purpose is to establish the maximum dollar and/or unit amount of a product line available to all firms within a specific defined area and period of time. It is the largest possible description of market size. The second variable is called the *market forecast;* its purpose is to establish the estimated dollar and/or unit sales of a product or product line for all firms within a certain defined area and period of time. In other words, market potential is units that could be sold, and market forecast is units that should be sold. One way to find the market forecast is to add up the competition's year-end sales numbers.

When figuring your market forecast, you need to ask yourself where you are in terms of its relationship to you. If the market is a place where you are *considering entering,* then you do not include your sales forecast. If it is a market that you are *currently in,* then you do include your sales forecast.

You should develop market size models for the total market area as well as by each target market. The full market size model is completed upon establishing your product's sales potential, sales forecasts, and market share. The model should display data that is linked to your products; this gives the reader a point of reference. You need to know (for product profitability reasons) how you might rate against the marketplace.

Format 10

Market Potential and Market Forcast

Last Three Years ($ thousands)

	19___ $	19___ Units	19___ $	19___ Units	Rate of Growth (%)	19___ $	19___ Units	Rate of Growth (%)
Market Potential								
Overall:	$5,760	2,880	$6,400	3,200	11	$7,040	3,520	11
Product:								
Product:								
Market Forecast								
Overall:	$575	315	$630	350	11	$780	420	20
Product:								
Product:								

Format 10 (Cont'd)

Next Three Years ($ thousands)

	19 ___		19 ___		Rate of Growth	19 ___		Rate of Growth
	$	Units	$	Units	(%)	$	Units	(%)
Market Potential								
Overall:								
Product:								
Product:								
Market Forecast								
Overall:								
Product:								
Product:								

MEASURING MARKET PENETRATION

All markets, mass or segmented, have parameters that must be understood in order to enter the market. Once in, direction and size must be quantified to determine where the market is headed in terms of the various shares claimed by current competitors and by the borders of the market itself. If you have already posted year-end sales figures, you can estimate your present and projected market share. Market share should be defined by each target market, by individual products, and by overall product line.

Barriers to Entry

Very few markets exist where marketers can get products into the marketplace quickly and painlessly. Each market has its own hurdles a business must master to enter and survive. One such hurdle is the market's structure. Its limitations establish what you can and cannot do in the marketplace. The other is learning how those limitations translate into problems that you will need to resolve.

Every market has limitations. For example, there may be specific time periods in which a product or service is required by the customer. A physical limitation, such as a faulty distribution channel, may also exist. In any case, the marketer needs to identify these limitations and determine their impact in the marketplace.

If the limitations can be minimized or eliminated, it may be beneficial for the marketer to take on the task. This requires careful consideration of both the benefits of opening the marketplace further and the liabilities of going through such a process. In effect, you must ask yourself if the positive results of overcoming barriers outweigh the negative elements that occur while attempting to do so.

Market Share Direction

The next step in defining how you could enter and impact the marketplace is to learn how much room for growth there is in the market. This means that you will address who owns the market and what they represent in terms of market share relative to the competition. The best way to understand how this works is through the example of dividing a pie. How is the pie cut? How many people want a slice? How big is the complete pie? The result is determining what you can expect out of the marketplace in terms of what is left. The market saturation point is when the combined shares will exhaust the available market potential.

To analyze anticipated growth, examine growth rates and patterns within the existing market. The objective is to measure fluctuation between the market area open for expansion and the collective market shares of your competitors. The following diagram illustrates this concept.

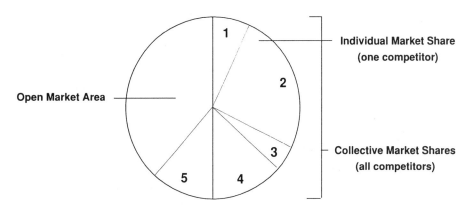

If the individual or collective market share is declining, the open area in your marketing pie will increase. This means more opportunity for your own growth. If the existing market participants are maintaining or increasing their shares of the pie, your product or service will have less of an opportunity to control a share of the market.

In addition to examining growth rates, you need to determine the market saturation point. This point is reached when the combined market shares of all competitors exhaust the market potential. You are not particularly concerned about where a product is in its life cycle at this point—you simply want to know when the availability of the market is likely to end.

The following model format will help you determine market saturation point. It is suggested that you look at five-year time periods for approximately 20 years. In come cases, the lifetime of a market may only be five years total. You can report your data in this model in terms of dollars or market percentage. Be sure to present the rationale upon which you figured your numbers. This will lend credibility to your estimates.

Format 11

Market Saturation Point as Indicated by Sales ($)

	Years					
	5	10	15	20	25	Total
Overall						
Product:	$1,000,000	$2,000,000	$1,500,000	$500,000	$1,000	
Product:						

The format on page 21 will help you look at market share relative to the entire market and relative to the competition. Normally, when measuring their market share, analysts compare themselves to their competitors. People like this method because it will produce large percentages even if you are a small player. A more accurate analysis of your market share, however, is to look at a comparison to the entire market. This will give you lower percentages but will be a better indicator of growth potential. Of course, market analysis based on both of these methods is the best choice.

ESTABLISHING KEY MARKET FACTORS

In assessing the entire market structure, it is important to understand its movements and changes. market factors tell you how the competition is positioned, alerts you to risks that the market brings, establishes where the market is in its life cycle, and identifies any sales fluctuations that have occurred because of changes in the marketplace.

Market Positioning

The purpose of market positioning is to determine how competitors are placed in the marketplace. Competitors' products are positioned in the marketplace based on their perception of the customer's wants and needs. These wants and needs are translated into market attributes. There are several methods marketers can use in determining the proper market attributes to be used in analyzing competitors' positioning strategies. There are many market positioning strategies that can be used, but regardless of which one you select, it must match the needs and wants of the customers. Possible strategies include positioning by usage, competition (pricing), alternatives, association, or matching (target market).

When collecting your research data regarding customer perceptions of currently available products, be sure to include the influencing factors that will determine that attributes used in the model.

Format 12

Market Share

Last Three Years — — —

Market Share (Relative to Market)

Overall:		*5%*	*1%*	*6%*	*3%*

Product:

Product:

Market Share (Relative to Competition)

Overall:		*43%*	*6%*	*47%*	*7%*

Product:

Product:

Next Three Years ($ thousands)	19 ___ Units	19 ___ Units	Rate of Growth (%)	19 ___ Units	Rate of Growth (%)

Market Share (Relative to Market)

Overall:

Product:

Product:

Market Share (Relative to Competition)

Overall:

Product:

Product:

$$\text{Market share relative to market} = \frac{\text{Market potential}}{\text{Year-end-sales}} \qquad \text{Market share relative to competition} = \frac{\text{Market forecast}}{\text{Year-end-sales}}$$

The following model is a perceptual map. It is designed to demonstrate positioning of products in your market. In this case, you are concerned with how competitors' products are positioned in the market as judged by factors of customer preference or perceptions.

The four sides represent product attributes: expensive/inexpensive, high quality/low quality. The numbers on the vertical and horizontal axes represent customer ranking of product desirability from a low of 1 to a high of 10. The letters a–h represent eight competitors currently in the market-place.

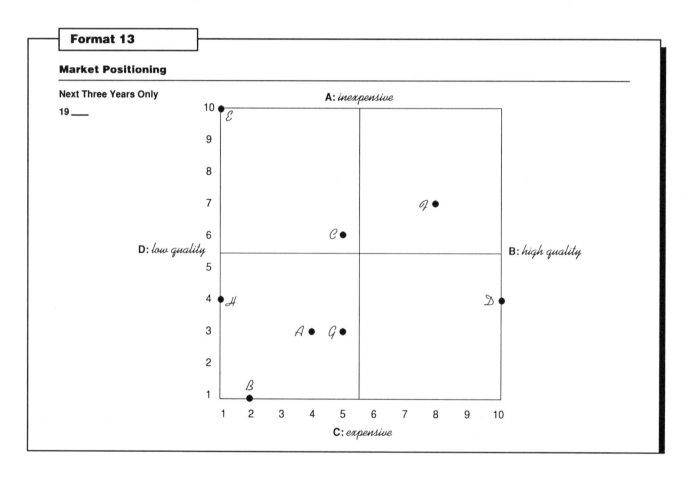

Format 13

Market Positioning

Next Three Years Only

19 ___

Quality	Price	Competitor
4	3	a
2	1	b
5	6	c
10	4	d
1	10	e
8	7	f
5	3	g
1	4	h

As you analyze these results, it becomes clear that Competitor F is in the best position. That competitor's product is relatively inexpensive and high-quality. Both product desirability characteristics are rated well by customers.

The perceptual map method allows you to see how customers perceive current offerings and highlights areas where your product may fit in to the marketing mix. Remember, it is not what you think that counts, it is what the customer perceives that will ensure your spot in the marketplace.

Summary of Key Risks

Each market has an element of risk. Your main objective is to translate a subjective situation into an objective determination of your chances of being successful or failing. The preferred method is to assess the market's risks by establishing development scenarios that may or may not materialize, based on a set of assumptions which are linked to changing variables or risk factors.

Market Life Cycle

Markets, like products, progress through life cycles. With markets, the stages of the life cycle are the same; it is the factors causing the stages to move through the various levels that are a bit different. These factors are time and customer availability, rather than sales. The other component to be addressed is a market's health, principally in financial terms. If a market is experiencing turmoil, it is less desirable.

The format below should be used to summarize markets from the past three years to the next three years.

There are four life cycle stages for markets:

- Introduction (new market/slow growth)

- Growth (recognized market/strong growth)

- Maturity (utilized market/steady growth)

- Decline (low-value market/weak growth)

Depending upon your needs, any one of the market life cycle stages can be attractive to you and beneficial for your particular product.

Format 14

Market Life Cycle

19 ——

Product	Market	Life Cycle Stage	Health
Brand X	#1	Growth	Stable
Brand Y	#2	Decline	Unstable

Market Fluctuations   Practically every market has some cycling due to seasonal change or other elements such as economic, cultural, or political events. Your goal is to try to establish how and to what degree they affect a market's sales performance levels. This will allow you to predict sales peaks and valleys.

By charting market fluctuations, you can track changes in the marketplace and in purchasing patterns. Such a chart may look like the following:

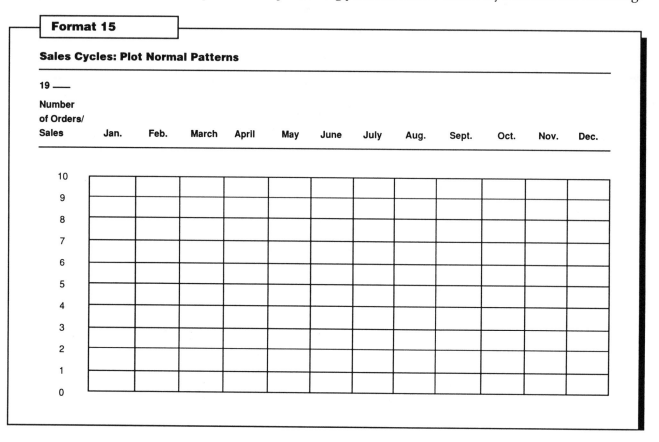

You can also use this type of chart to overlap sales data from your product in order to compare market sales patterns.

ASSESSING INDUSTRY STANDARDS   Determining the market's marketing standards is a key part of the analysis. It is here that a point of reference is established to give you a sense of how things are currently being run. If the standards being used are successful, there is little reason to reinvent the wheel. If the standards being used are unsuccessful, then perhaps new marketing strategies could be formed.

These standards are set by companies currently competing for business, as well as regulations and other restrictions. In evaluating the standards, it is important not only to determine what type of activities are being used, but also how effective those activities are. From these standards you can establish past, present, and future trends by examining the past three years and the next three years.

Marketing Research   The first step is to determine current industry standards and trends regarding the use of marketing research. Included in this should be marketing research activities (what you are doing now), product research activities (e.g., customer testing), and functional research activities (e.g., media tracking or customer satisfaction studies). Include the following in this section:

1. Budgets allocated

2. Research performed

3. Data collection and processing used

4. Results in the marketplace

Product Development   You will also need to discover what the industry standards and trends are regarding the management of product development. Included in this section should be strategies being used in offering products to the marketplace. Elements of this section should include the following:

1. Budgets allocated

2. Existing product line strategies used

3. New product line strategies used

4. Branding strategies used

5. Packaging used

Pricing   Next, you will need to determine the industry standards and trends regarding pricing policies. Included in this should be acceptable price levels and pricing incentives, such as volume discounts and gross margins. In addition, reasons for pricing changes, the frequency of such changes, control over costs, and historical pricing patterns need to be recognized. Be sure to include the following:

1. Budgets allocated

2. Price formulas used

3. Pricing strategies used

4. Price/cost/profit structure

The following model allows you to examine industry pricing averages. (Later, in the competition section, you will identify specific price structures.) To use the model, select a series of product types similar to yours that are competing in the market. Call that one Product A and call another Product B. Next, establish the average volume discount programs for

---

Format 16

Industry Pricing Averages: Profitability and Policy Structure

Volume (Units)	Product: *A*		Product: *B*	
	1–5	6–10	1–5	6–10
Base price ($)	500	500		
Discount ($)	0	10		
Revenue ($)	500	490		
Costs ($)	200	200		
Gross profit ($)	300	290		
Gross profit margin (%)	60	58		

each product. For example, is there a 10% discount for 1–3 units, a 20% discount for 4–10 units, etc. Based on the volume discount information and the average base price of the product, you can then figure the volume discount average, revenue, and costs of goods sold. The final two lines of the model provide a place for you to determine the average gross profit in dollars and the gross profit margin as a percentage.

Distribution

You will also need to determine the industry standards and trends for the usage of distribution channels. Included in this area should be the recognized avenues used in delivering products to the customer or the sales outlet. Items such as transportation, as well as distribution/marketing methods such as sales incentives and dealer financial and support package need to be established. Be sure to include the following in this section:

1. Budgets allocated

2. Channels used

Sales Management

The next step is to investigate the industry standards and trends for the methods used in selling and in managing sales. Included in this area should be the activities employed to generate sales, such as the length of sales cycle, types of sales forces used, sales tools and visual aids used in selling, sales incentives, territory design, and compensation/quota plans. The following items should be included in this section:

1. Budgets allocated

2. Size of sales force used

3. Internal sales promotions used

4. Compensations/quota plans used

5. Territories configured

Advertising

You will also need to ascertain the industry standards and trends for advertising. Included in this area should be media spending (with whom and how much), messages used, media used to communicate the message, reach/frequency/coverage, and principal influences. Be sure to include the following:

1. Budgets allocated

2. Message or themes used

3. Media used

The following format examines the advertising standards, by media type.

Format 17

Advertising Standards: Name and/or Types of Media

	19__	19__	19__
Direct:			
Mail	60% 130,000		
Phone			
Cable TV			
Interactive TV			
Video			
Fax			
Computer			
Outdoor:			
Billboard			
General signage			
Transit			
Television:			
Cable			

Format 17 (Cont'd)

Broadcast

    Home shopping

    Infomercials

Radio:

    Spot

Print:

    Newspaper

    Magazine

    Insert (FSI)

    Brochures

    Yellow Pages

Promotion Trends

The next step is to determine the industry standards and trends regarding promotions. Included in this area should be activities such as sales promotion spending, sponsorships used, trade shows attended, and event participation. The following items should be included:

1. Budgets allocated

2. Message or theme used

3. Activities and events used

Use the following format to collect this information for the past three years and the next three years.

Format 18

Promotion Standards: Name and/or Types of Media

	19__	19__	19__
Campaigns:			
Sports			
Community projects			
Sponsorship:			
Event	*10% 1,800,000*		
Place			
Individual			

Format 18 (Cont'd)

Merchandising:

Endorsements/licensing

Catalog

Sales promotions (for customers):

Floor displays

POP

Rebates/coupons

Special:

Trade shows

Public Relations

You will also need to establish the industry standards and trends for public relations. Included in this area should be activities such as techniques used for promoting positive images, as well as publicity and media relations policies. Be sure to include the following:

1. Budgets allocated

2. Message or theme used

3. Media strategies used

4. Activities or events used

Legal

The final step in this section is to determine the industry standards and trends for legal activities, such as proper positioning on legislative issues, relations with government agencies, and monitoring and influencing pending and existing legislation. The following items should be included:

1. Budgets allocated

2. Laws or regulations monitored

IDENTIFYING SECONDARY TARGET MARKETS

Secondary markets are nearly always available and should be considered. Secondary markets develop because of primary market resource limitations, new market growth, and organizational challenges. As a result, after you have selected your primary market, you should identify secondary or alternative markets. Segment numbers in the sample format represent market profiles selected in Formats 9 and 10.

Defining Secondary Target Markets by Product

To define a secondary market for future consideration by product, select a desired profile segment by defined trade areas, using the product as a method for additional market penetration. Record your data in format 19.

Defining Secondary Target Markets by Geography

To define a secondary market for future consideration by geographic area, select a desired profile segment by defined trade areas, using geography as a method for additional market penetration. Record your data in format 20.

Defining Secondary Target Markets by Customer

To define a secondary market for future consideration by customer type, select a desired profile segment by defined trade areas, using customer type as a method for additional market penetration. Record your data in format 21.

Formats 19, 20, and 21

Defining Secondary Target Markets

	Segment (Market Profile)			
	1	2	3	4
Secondary				
Tertiary				

Unit 2

Profiling Your Customers

IDENTIFYING YOUR CUSTOMERS

Understanding who your customers are, why they buy, where they buy, and how often they buy may be the most important marketing knowledge you ever possess. Marketing is far more exact than people realize, but it will never be completely exact because of the element of human behavior. This one element is the most difficult variable to judge and predict. You must identify specifically who your customers will be and then define their needs, wants, and desires. Once this is done, you can better determine how to reach them and acquire them as your customers. Once again, you may want to identify your customers by your product or product line to give you a reference point.

In the market segmentation section, segment profiles are established in an overall form by using various attributes and variables. In the consumer market environment, you use many of those same components in establishing who your customers are, except now you are identifying an actual person, place, or thing, not a profile or cluster. As a result, the customer ID in the market analysis means defining the actual individual types of customers, either as one type or a range of types.

Exhibit 2–1 illustrates how the customer profiling process links with the entire market definition process.

REASONS FOR PURCHASES

Once you have identified your customers, the next step is to establish how they make the decision to purchase your products, where they are most likely you buy your product, when they are likely to buy your product, how often they buy your product, and how much of your product they will buy. Assessing a customer's value for a particular product is difficult; the trick is identifying how the product satisfies a need or solves a problem. Then you will evaluate your customers' purchasing power to measure how often a customer may make purchases; this information can help you predict sales fluctuations. You should also determine the customer's purchase decision process and what influences their purchases. (See Exhibit 2–2.) The ultimate goal is to measure customers' shopping patterns by where they shop and link this information with what they buy and why. It is important to identify where shopping activities occur, whether near customers' workplaces or residential neighborhoods.

EXHIBIT 2–1
Market Identification and the Customer Profiling Process

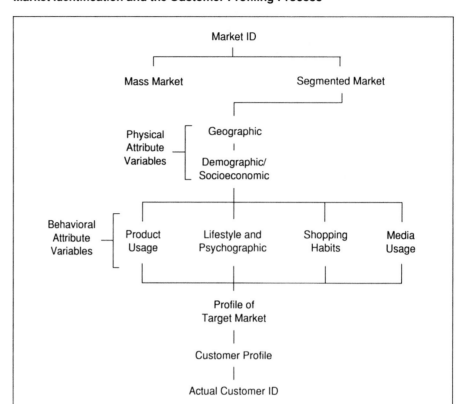

Format 22

Customer Definition

Product: ————————————

Target Market:	#1		#2	
Customer:	Primary	Secondary	Primary	Secondary
Description				
	Hispanic, males, 35–50 yrs. old	Hispanic, males' wives, 35–50 yrs. old	White, males, 35–50 yrs. old	White, males' wives, 35–50 yrs. old

---

Need Identification   There are many important elements to consider in defining the market-place, but the bottom line is customer needs. Whether customers' needs are currently being satisfied by some source or are not being satisfied, or

EXHIBIT 2-2
Identifying Product Purchased and Product Location

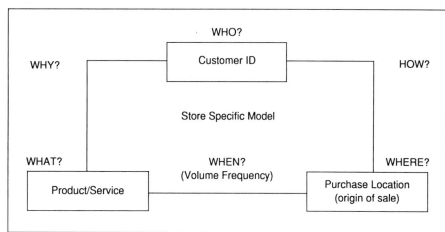

if customers are ready to have a need created for them, remember that customer needs are your number-one priority. The key elements in measuring need are customers' level of satisfaction and what motivates them to make purchases (quality, price, etc.).

Problem Identification

Once you understand the customers' needs, you then need to define why the need exists and how long it will last. The main point to understand, once again, is why a customer does or does not buy. In addition, what are the alternatives a customer could exercise in deciding whether to purchase or not to purchase? What are actual and/or potential solutions to problems?

Buying Behavior

The next step in defining customer factors is the area of understanding and perhaps predicting the element of buyer behavior. It is this element that causes marketing to be an inexact science; no matter how strong your marketing efforts are, the customer still has the ultimate power in deciding to buy. A key measurement of behavior is determining how much of a product a customer uses. The heavier the use level, the easier it is to understand customers' buying habits. The buying behavior to be charted includes the following:

1. Frequency (consumption patterns)

2. Volume per purchase

3. Reorders

4. Overall purchasing power

Customer purchasing power is a measurement of the ability of an individual or group to generate sales. The following model will allow you to track customer purchasing performance for the past three years and the next three years. For both primary and secondary markets, rate purchasing performance by frequency (how often a purchase is made) and by volume (how many units are purchased). You can then rate the customer performance by either or both of the criteria.

Format 23

Frequency and Volume of Purchases by Priority Customers

19 __

Product: _____	Frequency		Volume	
Customer ID	Low	High	Low	High
1. *Primary*		X ———————————— X		
2. *Secondary*		X ————— X		

Understanding the Purchase Decision Process	The next step is to isolate the actual act of purchasing. Although it is impossible to truly understand the final moments before a customer decides to purchase products, the process can be tracked and projected to some extent. The process a customer goes through when selecting a product is especially important, in the consumer market, where branding comes into play. Branding gives products an identity and gives the customer more options and issues to consider. Once you determine why they buy and when they buy, your understanding of how customers think about the product can be manipulated to impact favorably on a product	

Format 24

Purchasing Decision Variables

Brand Product: _____	Impulse (%)	Planned (%)	Loyal (%)	Complex (%)	Total
1. *Primary*	25%	25%	25%	25%	100%
2. *Primary*	30	40	20	10	100
3. *Secondary*	40	10	40	10	100
4. *Secondary*	35	15	40	10	100

purchase. Elements in understanding the purchase decision process include the following:

1. Length of sales cycle (How long does it take customers to buy?)

2. Impulse, planned, loyal, and complex purchase decisions

3. Timing (e.g., seasonal)

Purchasing Influences

With each purchase, something or someone influences a customer's decision to obtain or not to obtain a product. The trick is to try to identify the influencing forces governing the decision-making process. Once you have established the forces of purchasing influence (one or several), then you can assess how complex the market is. The more elements that impact a decision to purchase, the more difficult it will be to effectively control that market in terms of time, effort, and money. Types of purchasing influences to consider include the following:

1. Individual/group/parent/peer opinions

2. Price sensitivity

3. Personal preferences

4. Source of product information (e.g., media, friends, etc.)

Origin of Sale

In the consumer market, origin of sale is a key element in purchase motivation. This is because an individual makes the final decision to buy, and then physically seeks out the product and makes the actual transaction. Understanding the origin of sale tells you the point or reasoning behind purchasing a product. It tells you where and when customers are purchasing your products and what the most effective placement would be. Be sure to include the following in your analysis:

1. Point of purchase origin (type of store, outlet, etc.)

2. Point of delivery (if separate)

3. Point of product sale (motivation)

The following origin of sale model can be completed with research and/or scanner data that you have already obtained. Your objective here is to establish why customers buy and then match that data to your consumer types. For example, if you are relying on primary market research in the form of a survey, your questions could be designed to ask consumers to rank motivating factors on a scale from 1 to 5. If price was not a strong incentive to buy, the consumer would rank that factor as 1. (See the actual model for additional examples.)

To indicate customer purchase motivation patterns, select the element that most likely motivates a customer by placing a number between 1 and 10 (10 being the strongest) to determine importance. Once you determine

Format 25

Customer Purchase Motivation

Product	Price	Selection	Service	Quality/Appearance	Location
			Motivation to Buy		
1. Primary	1	4	2	3	5
2. Primary	5	3	2	1	4
3. Secondary	3	2	1	5	4

Format 26

Customer Sales*

Last Three Years / Next Three Years

19 ——

Product: ——————

	Primary			Secondary		
	dollars	units	%	dollars	units	%
Retail:						
Discount store	$3,000	1,000	10	$2,000	667	12
Department store	8,000	2,667	30	5,000	1,667	40
Specialty store	4,000	1,333	40	1,000	333	8
Variety store						
Supermarket						
Catalog showroom						
Convenience store						
Wholesale:						
Warehouse showroom						
Industrial distributors						
Special:						
Mail order						
Brokers						
Automatic/vending						
Door to door						
TV shopping						

Customer Type

* Dollars shown in millions

why a customer makes the decision to buy, you can identify where the customer completes the purchase. The Customer Sales model displays where customers shop according to type of store.

After you have established why and where a customer tends to buy, you can actually pinpoint the location where this purchasing behavior occurs. A method called "store specific analysis" uses new technology to help you track products based on the specific locations at which they were purchased. This data is generally obtained through scanner data vendors and can be recorded in a form such as the following.

Format 27

Store-specific Performance (Origin/Point of Sale)

Product/Brand	Customer Type/Composite	Store Location
Toothpaste/Crest	Primary	XYZ Market/10th & Main
Butter/Store's	Primary	XYZ Market/10th & Main
Soda/Canada Dry	Secondary	Fred's Market/32 E. Doe St.

You can now take the store you have identified and determine its trade/service area. Your first objective is to break down the area by priority markets and then match the address of the customer with the store location. This should help you determine if the connection between customer and location is based on the neighborhood or the attraction of the specific store. Remember, the more specific you can be about geographic levels, the more accurate your analysis becomes.

Format 28

Store-specific Location (Market/Trade Area)

Store/Location	Defined Area		
	Primary Block Level	Secondary Block Level	Tertiary Block Level
XYZ Market, 106 Main	38 blocks, 183 primary customers		
XY2 Market, 104 Main			
Fred's Market 32 E. Doe St.			

Customer Identification

At this point, total customer identification is possible by matching the customer identification and reasons for purchase (customer profile) with a customer database (current and potential) to create a customer list for marketing purposes.

To perform this match, compare your desired customer (as listed on the Customer Definition format) with a list of actual customers from your database. The following format can be used for this comparison and should serve as a basis for your data file.

Format 29

Customer ID Data File

Customer Profile Type	Actual Customer	
1. Customer variables:	1. Customer:	
a. *Hispanic*	a. Address:	*163 Hillside Dr., Chicago, IL 60621*
b. *Males*	b. Customer name:	*Pedro Valdez*
c. *35–50 years old*	c. Telephone number:	*202-312-8810*
2. Customer variables:	2. Customer:	
a. *White*	a. Address:	
b. *Males*	b. Customer name:	
c. *35–50 years old*	c. Telephone number:	

Unit 3

Analyzing Your Competition

IDENTIFYING YOUR COMPETITION

Understanding your competition's capabilities, resources, and strategies can help you pinpoint their vulnerabilities. Competition can manifest itself in many ways, such as a high-tech company that invents a new product for a new need. Although the need is new or there may be no other competitors in the marketplace, chances are that a customer is filling the need in some other way. You should also remember to identify competitors at different levels. For example, if you are an airline carrier, your competition is not only other airline carriers, but also all other forms of transportation (i.e., buses, automobiles, trains, etc.).

It is important to discover as much information as possible about your competition. However, obtaining the information may prove difficult because competitors do not freely share meaningful data. As a result, complete the following formats to the best of your ability with the information at hand.

The following model provides a method for identifying your competitor by product line and target market. Be sure to identify products at the various points of their life cycle. If they are in decline, they should be listed in the "Past" column. Active products go in the "Present" column. Products that are under development or have not yet reached market are classified as "Future."

Format 30

Competitor Identification

| Competitor | Product Line | | | Target Market/Customers |
	Past	Present	Future	
ABC Company		Brand X		20–35-year-old white females
XYZ Inc.			Brand Y	35–50-year-old white females

The next format identifies competitors by performance power in the marketplace. Each competitor should be identified by area of distribution (local, national, regional) and market share (in percent). Then rank them in order of importance to the market.

Format 31

Competition by Target Market

19___

Competitor	Ranking	Market Share	Distribution
Brand X	1st	50%	National
Brand Y	2nd	20	National

A third way to identify competitors is by sales and market share performance. You must first establish sales levels by looking at two variables: sales potential and sales forecast. Sales potential is based on the resources of a competitor and its ability to use those resources to meet the needs of its service area. Sales forecast is a measure of their current sales projections for coming years. When using either variable, examine current and past projections to gauge how well a competitor met its expectations. Use the following format for this analysis.

Format 32

Competitor Sales Performance ($ thousands)

Last Three Years

	19 — $	19 — Units	19 — $	19 — Units	Rate of Growth (%)	19 — $	19 — Units	Rate of Growth (%)
Sales Potential:								
Overall:	$100	1,000	$150	1050	5%	$200	1,200	14%
Product:								
Product:								
Sales Forecast:								
Overall:	60	600	85	850	42	120	999	18
Product:								
Product:								

Format 32 (Cont'd)

Next Three Years

	19 __		19 __		Rate of Growth (%)	19 __		Rate of Growth (%)
	$	Units	$	Units		$	Units	
Sales Potential:								
Overall:								
Product:								
Product:								
Sales Forecast:								
Overall:								
Product:								
Product:								

Format 33

Competitor Market Share ($ thousands)

Last Three Years

	19 __	Units	19 __	Units	Rate of Growth (%)	19 __	Units	Rate of Growth (%)
Market Share (Relative to Market):								
Overall:					8%			9%
Product:								
Product:								
Market Share (Relative to Competition):								
Overall:					52			52
Product:								
Product:								

Format 33 (Cont'd)

Next Three Years

	19 ___	Units	19 ___	Units	Rate of Growth (%)	19 ___	Units	Rate of Growth (%)
Market Share (Relative to Market):								
Overall:								
Product:								
Product:								
Market Share (Relative to Competition):								
Overall:								
Product:								
Product:								

MEASURING THE COMPETITION'S STRENGTHS AND WEAKNESSES

Competitive Advantages of Competitors

Once you have established who the players are in the marketplace and what impact they have on that marketplace, then you need to assess each one to determine its strengths and weaknesses. In measuring each one's strengths, you will need to determine four basic elements that can give you a profile of what they do well now and what they can do to better themselves in the future.

A: Ability to satisfy customers' needs and desires

B: Track record and reputation

C: Staying power (financial resources)

D: Key personnel

To this point, the information you have used to identify the competition has been very quantitative. This model allows you to write qualitative, narrative information about each competitor's abilities.

Competitive Disadvantages of Competitors

In measuring weaknesses, you will try to identify what the competition cannot do well, or at least areas that may be open to problems. The same four elements used to assess strengths can help you assess your competitors' weaknesses. Having the same four elements as a measurement will help you achieve a balanced viewpoint.

A: Ability to satisfy customers' needs and desires

B: Track record and reputation

Format 34

Competitive Advantages of Competitors

Competitor	Strengths			
	A	B	C	D
Brand X	Seems to satisfy customer needs moderately. Strength comes as a result of ease of usage, low price, and advertising.	Has a long and strong history of quality. Customers treat it as a reliable old stand-by.	Parent company just went public, giving them a lot of new cash flow.	Product manager has been at her job for 20 years and knows the business.
Brand Y	Satisfies customer needs better than Brand X by being better and faster.	Replacing a product that was very successful. Is new and has a limited track record.	Owned by XYZ, Inc., which is a secure, expanding, family-owned business.	R&D staff is excellent and is always looking to improve products.

C: Staying power (financial resources)

D: Key personnel

Using the following format, write qualitative, narrative descriptions of the competition's disadvantages.

Format 35

Competitive Advantages of Competitors

Competitor	Weaknesses			
	A	B	C	D

EVALUATING MARKETING STRATEGIES

Profitability and Financial Structure

The third area of focus is evaluating competitors' marketing strategies. Unlike the marketing mix industry standards section, which collectively measures all competitors, regulators, and customers by establishing industry norms, averages, and ranges, this section deals with each competitor individually and pinpoints each one's approach to marketing.

The first element of measurement is a competitor's level of profitability. Items such as gross profit margins, gross profit/income levels, return on investment, and cost of marketing are all areas to be determined. Your biggest hurdle will be in obtaining this sensitive information regarding a competitor. If you can get the information, these data are extremely valuable.

The following format can be used to illustrate elements of a competitor's profitability level. Again, you will only be able to use as much of this form as you have information to support it.

Format 36

Profitability and Financial Structure

19——

Competitor: _____ Brand X _____

Overall Product Line (Year Ending/Past):

Sales ($)	$200,000
Sales (Units)	$1,200
Rate of growth (%)	14%
Cost of goods sold	$100,000
Gross profit	$100,000
Gross margin	50%

Product (Year Ending/Future):

Sales ($)	
Sales (Units)	
Rate of growth (%)	
Cost of goods sold	
Gross profit	
Gross margin	

It sounds overly simplified, but if a product can't be produced and sold at a price that covers cost of production, generates profit, and is not attractive to customers, the product is unmarketable. In analyzing your competition's ability to sell a marketable product, you need to know their cost and price structuring. The following model is the same as the one you used in the Industry Standards section. Complete it as before, but use information on the competitor's pricing structure.

Format 37

Pricing/Cost Structure

19___

Competitor: _____ *Brand X* _____

Volume (Units)	Product			Product	
	1–5	6–10	11–15	1–5	5+
Price ($)	$167	$167			
Discount ($)	0	20			
Revenue ($)	167	147			
Costs ($)	84	64			
Gross profit ($)	83	63			

In analyzing profitability, it is also important to examine marketing expenses. This key component, commonly called "cost of marketing" or "cost of sales," is an additional method of viewing a competitor's ability to produce marketable products. The following model asks you to identify how much a competitor is spending and how that amount relates to the percent of products sold.

Format 38

Marketing Expenses by Competitor

Marketing Function	19___ ($)	Percentage of Total Sales	19___ ($)	Percentage of Total Sales	Percentage Change of Allocated Dollars
Marketing research	5,000	2.5	4,000	2.0	<20.0>
Product/new product development	3,000	1.5	2,000	1.0	<33.3>
Pricing	0	0	0	0	0
Distribution	5,000	2.5	6,000	3.0	20.0
Sales	10,000	5.0	11,000	5.5	10.0
Advertising	8,500	4.3	10,000	5.0	17.7
Promotions	6,000	3.0	8,000	4.0	33.3
Public relations	500	0.3	0	0	<100.0>
Legal	2,000	1.0	1,000	0.5	<50.0>
Total	40,000	—	42,000	—	5.0
Percentage of sales	20%	20.1	21%	21.0	—

Format 39

Media Usage Expenses by Competitor

	19 __ ($)	Percent of Total Advertising Budget	19 __ ($)	Percent of Total Advertising Budget	19 __ ($)	Total
Direct response:						
Mail	—	—	2,000	20		2,000
Phone	—	—	1,000	10		1,000
Cable TV	—	—	—	—		—
Interactive TV	—	—	—	—		—
Video	—	—	—	—		—
Fax	—	—	—	—		—
Computer	—	—	—	—		—
Outdoor response:						
Billboard	—	—	—	—		—
General signage	—	—	—	—		—
Transit	—					
Television viewership:						
Cable	1,500	17.0	1,500	15.0		3,000
Broadcast	—	—	—	—		—
Home shopping	—	—	—	—		—
Infomercials	—	—	—	—		—
Radio listenership:						
Spot	4,000	47.0	1,000	10.0		5,000
Print readership:						
Newspaper	2,000	24.0	1,000	10.0		3,000
Magazine	—	—	2,000	20.0		2,000
Insert (FSI)	—	—	—	—		—
Yellow Pages	1,000	12.0	1,000	10.0		2,000
Special viewership:						
Sports	—	—	—	—		0
POP	—	—	500	5.0		500
Floor displays	—	—	—	—		—
Coupons	—	—	—	—		—
Sales premiums	—	—	—	—		—
Total	$8,500	100	$10,000	100		$18,500

A media usage expense analysis is a tool to extract the advertising expenses from an overall budget. The model on page 46 provides you with an example of how a competitor may use advertising. Advertising costs tabulated on this format should include such things as production/creation and media placement/buying. The data are displayed as a dollar amount and as a percentage of the total advertising budget.

Research and Development Activities

The next step will be to find out what new products are currently in the pipeline with competitors in the marketplace and to determine whether there are companies that could become new competitors as a result of new product introductions. Once again, obtaining this information is difficult because competitors are even more secretive about these activities than about their profits. However, usually competitors can only keep quiet about their products in the initial stages; once they begin testing their secrets, they become harder to protect.

Format 40

Research and Development Activities

19___

Competitor	Stage	Release Date	Impact
XK-1000	Prototype	June '93	Replacement of product
20001-A	Test market	April '93	All new product

Opportunity Projections

As an extension of the research and development activities section, it is vital to understand how new developments will translate into market opportunities for you. How long will your window of opportunity be open before your initial success breeds new competition? How would competitors' products compare with yours? These questions are just a sample of the issues you need to resolve. The model on page 48 will help you complete this analysis.

Format 41

Opportunity Projections

19 —

New Competitors	Products	Estimated Base Price	Features/Benefits
Top Gun, Inc.	XK-1000	$170	Time-saving
AAAA Corp.	20001-A	200	Multipurpose

Barriers to Entry into the Market

As you evaluate the marketplace to determine whether you want to enter it, you also need to assess competitors' ability to enter the market and survive. Barriers to entering a market consist of several elements, but generally they are linked to cost, especially in terms of investment cost. The goal is to see if competitors are experiencing the barriers you've witnessed and to what degree they are dealing with those barriers.

A: Time

B: Technology

C: Key personnel

D: Customer limitations (brand loyalty, existing relationships)

E: Existing patents and trademarks

Format 42

Competitors' Barriers to Entry

Competitor	A. Time	B. Technology	C. Key Personnel	D. Customer Limitations	E. Existing Patents and Trademarks
Brand X	Their window of opportunity is estimated to be 6 months, beginning 2 months from now. However, they may not be in their new factory in time to produce and bring the product to market.	The technology they are using is outdated and although it works, it will never let Brand X perform at the level it should.	They have very loyal workers who are flexible. The result is that they can be counted on to adjust to market demands in terms of production scheduling.	Customers feel very good about the product and are willing to accept change.	No violation of patents.
Brand Y	Because their product is new, their timing is perfect. They are positioned to hit the ground running.	Brand Y is built on a whole new platform; as a result it is not only able to meet current market needs but can be expanded.	Key people are missing in the service/support area. Without these people, pushing a new product onto the market may create a major problem.	Previous customers of Brand Y were not very loyal. As a result, there is some question if customers will risk trying and using this product on a regular basis.	No violations of patents.

Unit 4

Working within Regulatory Restrictions

FEDERAL, STATE, AND LOCAL GOVERNMENT REGULATIONS

Almost every market is regulated in some way. Not understanding the rules of the game and not working within those rules can destroy your marketing efforts. An example would be if you launched a new consumer product and discovered after the product had been out for several weeks that a new law had been passed or a new technology was licensed that either forced you to retool the product or would eliminate it altogether. Such a mistake would prove to be very costly. Knowing what to expect can help you determine the market's future.

Government Regulations

The first area of restrictions is usually government regulations. A government agency that administers laws, rules, and regulations is set up to control a market and keep it safe and fair for all. The goal is to identify any and all requirements established by government, identify the various government agencies that oversee market actions, and determine your costs of complying. The following elements should be considered:

1. Approval (e.g., F.D.A.)

2. Special tax situation

3. Consumer labeling/packaging awareness (e.g., F.T.C.)

4. Purchase limitations

Laws That Affect the Product's Existence

In addition to existing laws, rules, and regulations, you need to be aware of impending changes to those laws, rules, and regulations as well as completely new laws, rules, and regulations that are being considered. It is not enough to try to understand and comply with the present legal situation. Pending legislations can affect a market negatively or positively.

Format 43

Laws/Rules/Regulations

Product	Past	Current	Future	Agency/Legislative Control
Your Product 1		*x*		*FTC*
Your Product 2		*x*	*x*	*FDA/FTC*

OTHER MARKET LIMITATIONS

Anticipated Market Changes

Other than laws, rules, and regulations, there are basic market limitations based on factors inherent to the market environment structure. You will need to identify the various factors that impact the market and determine their influence and how they can be changed. Be sure to consider the following:

1. Economic factors

2. Cultural factors

3. Technological factors

4. Political factors

5. Time factors

6. Suppliers

Format 44

Anticipated Market Changes

Product	Factor Type	Effect on Market
Your Product 1	*Cultural*	*Hispanic community acceptance*
Your Product 2	*Economic*	*Customers are unemployed/low-income*

MEETING REQUIREMENTS AND MAKING CHANGES

Once you have established what it will take to conform to the market's requirements, you must then assess what the cost will be and whether it is worth the effort to invest to make the necessary adjustments. You must also determine what it will take to meet the market requirements. You will also need to define the options that are open.

Timing Involved in Meeting the Requirements

The time it will take to meet market requirements is very important for projecting costs and resource allocations. How long it takes you to comply with these changes will once again tell you the amount of effort it will take to exist in the marketplace.

Cost of Meeting the Requirements

The cost of meeting market requirements is the bottom-line issue. You should go into great detail to determine how much it will cost in real dollars to comply with requirements before entering the market.

Format 45

Cost of Meeting Market Requirements

Product	Restriction	Timing	Cost to comply
Your Product 1	Federal law	6 months	$15,000 (filing and legal fees)
Your Product 2	Economic	no limit	does not apply

Unit 5

Comparing Your Market Analysis with Existing Market Research

EVALUATING EXISTING MARKETING STUDIES

Many marketing studies have probably been performed for your target markets by competitors, investment bankers, private research firms, and others. These data may be relevant to your market analysis. If possible, those research sources should be tapped to check against your findings and to further define the market.

The following items should be considered in determining the value of existing marketing research data:

- Who compiled and published the report?

- When was the study performed?

- How many sources were used?

- Where was this study performed?

- Why was the study conducted, and who paid for it?

- What were the results and who benefited from those results?

- How do the findings compare with your findings?

- Are adjustments needed or should more marketing research be performed?

ADJUSTING YOUR MARKET ANALYSIS

After you have completed your market analysis and compared your findings and analysis with other findings, you may need to make changes to your market analysis. You may need to perform more research or go back through your analysis and verify your data. It is always better to at least review other approaches and results to get an objective viewpoint in this very subjective science.

At the end of the market analysis, it is important that you try to assess the degree of demand in the marketplace. It is a very difficult assignment to place a value in a quantitative or qualitative formula. There is almost always a need for a product in every market; the key is recognizing the difference between need and demand. You make money with demand, not need.

Format 46

Degree of Marketplace Demand

Product	Previous Marketing Studies	Date	Findings	Adjustments (If any)
Your Product 1	Hopkins research marketing study	1989	Strong value placed on educating consumer	Review legal concerns
Your Product 2	No studies	—	—	—

Part 2

Data Reporting: Formats

After you have input and processed the marketing data, the next step is to place that information in a format suitable for presentation. There is no need to include these exact formats in your final document; instead, a solid market analysis blends written narrative segments with matrix models and charts containing hard data. This breaks up the data being presented and gives the reader a sense of a beginning and an end.

Identifying Your Markets

Formats 1–21 should be used to help you identify your potential target markets. See Unit 1 in Part 1 for explanations and examples of the formats.

Format 1

Geographic Variables in Market Segmentation

	Defined Area	
Levels (Standard Unit)	**Selection**	**Represents**
Global/International	_____	_____
National	_____	_____
Regional	_____	_____
Divisional	_____	_____
State	_____	_____
County	_____	_____
Minor Civil Division/ Census County Division (e.g., townships)	_____	_____
Places (city and town)	_____	_____
Census Tract/Block Numbering Area (population)	_____	_____
Block Group	_____	_____
Block	_____	_____
Street		
Place of Residence/ Place of Business	_____	_____

Format 2

Demographic/Socioeconomic Variables in Market Segmentation

Overall Area (Universe): _____

Defined Area (Target): _____

Descriptor	Defined Area		Overall Area		Index (%)
	Units	%	Units	%	

Sex:

Male

Female

Age distribution:

Marital status:

Format 2 (Continued)

Demographic/Socioeconomic Variables in Market Segmentation

Overall Area (Universe): _____

Defined Area (Target): _____

	Defined Area		Overall Area		
Descriptor	**Units**	**%**	**Units**	**%**	**Index (%)**

Education (last grade attended):

Occupation:

Format 2 (Continued)

Demographic/Socioeconomic Variables in Market Segmentation

Overall Area (Universe): _____

Defined Area (Target): _____

Descriptor	Defined Area		Overall Area		Index (%)
	Units	%	Units	%	

Ethnic classification:

Annual household income:

Household producers:

Demographic/Socioeconomic Variables in Market Segmentation

Overall Area (Universe): _____

Defined Area (Target): _____

Descriptor	Defined Area		Overall Area		Index (%)
	Units	%	Units	%	

Size of household:

Householder status:

Type of housing unit:

Lived in area:

Total

Format 3

Product Usage Variables in Market Segmentation

Product Comparison Type: _____

Overall Area (Universe): _____

Defined Area (Target): _____

Descriptor	Defined Area		Overall Area		Index (%)
	Units	%	Units	%	
Heavy:					
Medium:					
Light:					
Total					

Format 4

Lifestyle Variables in Market Segmentation

Overall Area (Universe): _____

Defined Area (Target): _____

	Defined Area		Overall Area		
Descriptor	**Units**	**%**	**Units**	**%**	**Index (%)**

Restaurant preferences:

Leisure-time activities:

Health care usage:

Banking/financial affairs:

Auto ownership:

Total

Format 5

Psychographic Variables in Market Segmentation

Overall Area (Universe): _____

Defined Area (Target): _____

Descriptor (Group ID)	Defined Area		Overall Area		
	Units	%	Units	%	Index (%)
Upper crust					
Lap of luxury					
Established wealth					
Total					

Format 6

Shopping Habits Variables in Market Segmentation

Overall Area (Universe): _____

Defined Area (Target): _____

Descriptor	Defined Area		Overall Area		
	Units	%	Units	%	Index (%)
Retail store preference:					
Department store					
Specialty store					
Supermarket					
Convenience store					
Shopping Motivation:					
Price					
Selection					
Service					
Quality					
Location of store					
Purchase patterns:					
Store					
Catalog/direct mail					
TV shopping					
Cash/check					
Credit card					
Coupon					
Brand label					
Major purchase intentions:					
Car/truck					
Computer					
Furniture					
Appliances					
Home					
Leisure					
College education					
Electronics					
Total					

Format 7

Media Usage Variables (by Medium Used)

Overall Area (Universe): _____

Defined Area (Target): _____

Descriptor	Defined Area Units	%	Overall Area Units	%	Index (%)
Direct:					
Mail					
Phone					
Outdoor:					
Billboard					
Transit					
Television:					
Cable					
Broadcast					
Radio:					
Spot					
Print:					
Newspaper					
Magazine					
Insert (FSI)					
Special:					
Yellow Pages					
Total					

Format 8

Target Market Formulation

Target Market				
1		**2**		**3**
Descriptors	**Counts**	**Descriptors**	**Counts**	
Total				

Format 9

Evaluating the Attractiveness of Each Profile Segment

Target Market

1		2		3
Qualify				
Descriptors	**Counts**	**Descriptors**	**Counts**	
Total				

Target Market

3(#1)		2(#2)		1(#3)
Prioritize				
Descriptors	**Counts**	**Descriptors**	**Counts**	
Total				

Format 10

Market Potential and Market Forecast

Last Three Years ($ thousands)

	19___		19___		Rate of Growth	19___		Rate of Growth
	$	Units	$	Units	(%)	$	Units	(%)
Market Potential								
Overall:								
Product:								
Product:								
Product:								
Product:								
Product:								
Market Forecast								
Overall:								
Product:								
Product:								
Product:								
Product:								
Product:								

Format 10 (Continued)

Market Potential and Market Forecast

Next Three Years ($ thousands)

	19 ___		19 ___		Rate of Growth	19 ___		Rate of Growth
	$	Units	$	Units	(%)	$	Units	(%)
Market Potential								
Overall:								
Product:								
Product:								
Product:								
Product:								
Product:								
Market Forecast								
Overall:								
Product:								
Product:								
Product:								
Product:								
Product:								

Format 11

Market Saturation Point as Indicated by Sales ($)

	Years					
	5	**10**	**15**	**20**	**25**	**Total**
Overall						
Product:						
Product:						
Product:						
Product:						
Product:						
Product:						
Product:						
Product:						
Product:						
Product:						
Product:						
Product:						

Format 12

Market Share

Last Three Years

	19 ___ Units	19 ___ Units	Rate of Growth (%)	19 ___ Units	Rate of Growth (%)
Market Share (Relative to Market)					
Overall:					
Product:					
Product:					
Product:					
Product:					
Product:					
Market Share (Relative to Competition)					
Overall:					
Product:					
Product:					
Product:					
Product:					
Product:					

Format 12 (Continued)

Market Share

Next Three Years

	19 ___ Units	19 ___ Units	Rate of Growth (%)	19 ___ Units	Rate of Growth (%)
Market Share (Relative to Market)					
Overall:					
Product:					
Product:					
Product:					
Product:					
Product:					
Market Share (Relative to Competition)					
Overall:					
Product:					
Product:					
Product:					
Product:					
Product:					

Format 13

Market Positioning

Last Three Years

19 _____

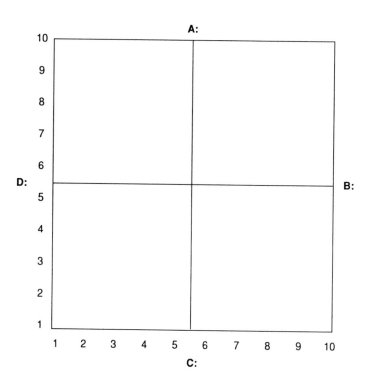

A:

B:

C:

D:

Format 13 (Continued)

Market Positioning

Last Three Years

19 ___

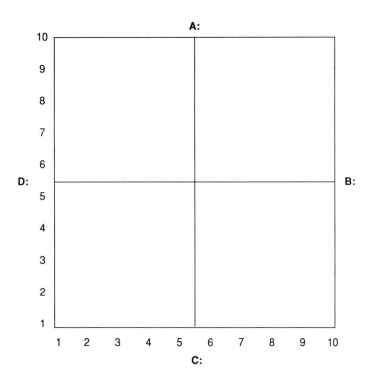

A:

B:

C:

D:

Format 13 (Continued)

Market Positioning

Last Three Years

19 ____

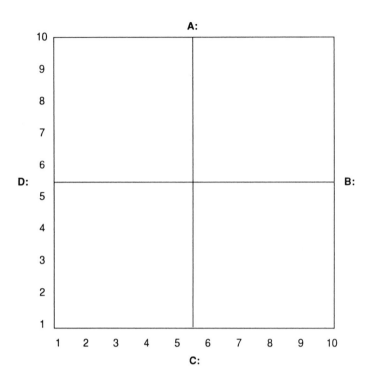

A:

B:

C:

D:

Format 13 (Continued)

Market Positioning

Next Three Years

19 ___

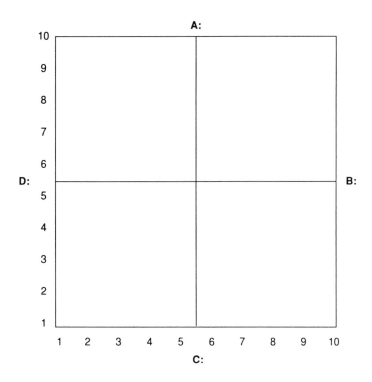

A:

B:

C:

D:

Format 13 (Continued)

Market Positioning

Next Three Years

19 _____

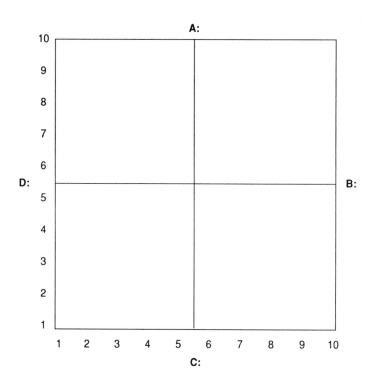

A:

B:

C:

D:

Format 13 (Continued)

Market Positioning

Next Three Years

19 ___

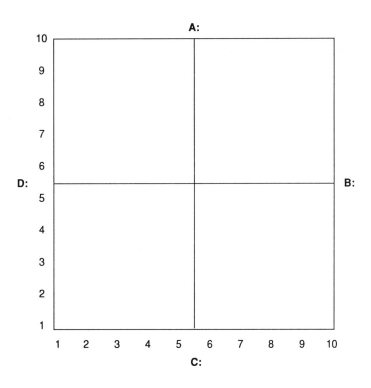

A:

B:

C:

D:

Format 14

Market Life Cycle

Last Three Years

19 ——

Product	Market	Life Cycle Stage	Health

19 ——

Product	Market	Life Cycle Stage	Health

19 ——

Product	Market	Life Cycle Stage	Health

Format 14 (Continued)

Market Life Cycle

Next Three Years

19 ——

Product	Market	Life Cycle Stage	Health

19 ——

Product	Market	Life Cycle Stage	Health

19 ——

Product	Market	Life Cycle Stage	Health

Format 15

Sales Cycles: Plot Normal Patterns

Last Three Years

19 ____

**Number
of Orders/
Sales**

	Jan.	Feb.	March	April	May	June	July	Aug.	Sept.	Oct.	Nov.	Dec.
10												
9												
8												
7												
6												
5												
4												
3												
2												
1												
0												

Format 15 (Continued)

Sales Cycles: Plot Normal Patterns

Last Three Years

19 ___

**Number
of Orders/
Sales**

	Jan.	Feb.	March	April	May	June	July	Aug.	Sept.	Oct.	Nov.	Dec.
10												
9												
8												
7												
6												
5												
4												
3												
2												
1												
0												

Sales Cycles: Plot Normal Patterns

Last Three Years

19 ____

Number of Orders/ Sales	Jan.	Feb.	March	April	May	June	July	Aug.	Sept.	Oct.	Nov.	Dec.
10												
9												
8												
7												
6												
5												
4												
3												
2												
1												
0												

Format 15 (Continued)

Sales Cycles: Plot Normal Patterns

Next Three Years

19 ___

**Number
of Orders/
Sales**   Jan.   Feb.   March   April   May   June   July   Aug.   Sept.   Oct.   Nov.   Dec.

	Jan.	Feb.	March	April	May	June	July	Aug.	Sept.	Oct.	Nov.	Dec.
10												
9												
8												
7												
6												
5												
4												
3												
2												
1												
0												

Format 15 (Continued)

Sales Cycles: Plot Normal Patterns

Next Three Years

19 ___

**Number
of Orders/
Sales**

	Jan.	Feb.	March	April	May	June	July	Aug.	Sept.	Oct.	Nov.	Dec.
10												
9												
8												
7												
6												
5												
4												
3												
2												
1												
0												

Format 15 (Continued)

Sales Cycles: Plot Normal Patterns

Next Three Years

19 ___

Number of Orders/ Sales	Jan.	Feb.	March	April	May	June	July	Aug.	Sept.	Oct.	Nov.	Dec.
10												
9												
8												
7												
6												
5												
4												
3												
2												
1												
0												

Format 16

Industry Pricing Averages: Profitability and Policy Structure

	Product	Product
Volume (Units)		
Base price ($)		
Discount ($)		
Revenue ($)		
Costs ($)		
Gross profit ($)		
Gross profit margin (%)		

Format 17

Advertising Standards: Name and/or Types of Media

	19 __	19 __	19 __
Direct:			
Mail			
Phone			
Cable TV			
Interactive TV			
Video			
Fax			
Computer			
Outdoor:			
Billboard			
General signage			
Transit			
Television:			
Cable			
Broadcast			
Home shopping			
Infomercials			
Radio:			
Spot			
Print:			
Newspaper			
Magazine			
Insert (FSI)			
Brochures			
Yellow Pages			

Format 18

Promotion Standards: Name and/or Types of Media

	19 __	19 __	19 __
Campaigns:			
Sports			
Community projects			
Sponsorship:			
Event			
Place			
Individual			
Merchandising:			
Endorsements/licensing			
Catalog			
Sales promotions (for customers):			
Floor displays			
POP			
Rebates/coupons			
Special:			
Trade shows			

Format 19

Secondary Target Markets Defined by Product

	Segment (Market Profile)			
	1	2	3	4

Secondary

Tertiary

Format 20

Secondary Target Markets Defined by Geography

	Segment (Market Profile)			
	1	2	3	4

Secondary

Tertiary

Format 21

Secondary Target Markets Defined by Customer

	Segment (Market Profile)			
	1	2	3	4
Secondary				

Tertiary

Profiling Your Customers

Formats 22–29 should be used to help you profile your current and prospective customers. See Unit 2 in Part 1 for explanations and examples of the formats.

Format 22

Customer Definition

Product: _____

Target Market: #*1*   #*2*
                                        _____   _____

Customer: **Primary**   **Secondary**   **Primary**   **Secondary**

Description

Format 23

Frequency and Volume of Purchases by Priority Customers

Last Three Years

19 ___

Product: _____	Frequency		Volume	
Customer ID*	**Low**	**High**	**Low**	**High**
1.				
2.				

* Ranked in order of importance, beginning with the most important customer.

Format 23 (Continued)

Frequency and Volume of Purchases by Priority Customers

Last Three Years

19 ___

Product: _____	Frequency		Volume	
Customer ID*	**Low**	**High**	**Low**	**High**

1.

2.

* Ranked in order of importance, beginning with the most important customer.

Format 23 (Continued)

Frequency and Volume of Purchases by Priority Customers

Last Three Years

19 ___

Product: _____	Frequency		Volume	
Customer ID*	**Low**	**High**	**Low**	**High**

1.

2.

* Ranked in order of importance, beginning with the most important customer.

Format 23 (Continued)

Frequency and Volume of Purchases by Priority Customers

Next Three Years

19 ___

Product: _____		Frequency			Volume	
Customer ID*		Low	High		Low	High

1.

2.

---

* Ranked in order of importance, beginning with the most important customer.

Format 23 (Continued)

Frequency and Volume of Purchases by Priority Customers

Next Three Years

19 ___

Product: _____	Frequency		Volume	
Customer ID*	**Low**	**High**	**Low**	**High**

1.

2.

* Ranked in order of importance, beginning with the most important customer.

Format 23 (Continued)

Frequency and Volume of Purchases by Priority Customers

Next Three Years

19 ___

Product: _____	Frequency		Volume	
Customer ID*	**Low**	**High**	**Low**	**High**

1.

2.

* Ranked in order of importance, beginning with the most important customer.

Format 24

Purchasing Decision Variables

Brand Product: _____

	Impulse (%)	Planned (%)	Loyal (%)	Complex (%)	Total
1.					
2.					
3.					
4.					

Format 25

Customer Purchase Motivation

Product	Motivation to Buy				
	Price	Selection	Service	Quality/Appearance	Location

Format 26

Customer Sales*

Last Three Years

19 ___

Product: _____

	Customer Type					
	Primary			Secondary		
	dollars	units	%	dollars	units	%
Retail:						
Discount store						
Department store						
Specialty store						
Variety store						
Supermarket						
Catalog showroom						
Convenience store						
Wholesale:						
Warehouse showroom						
Industrial distributor						
Special:						
Mail order						
Brokers						
Automatic/vending						
Door to door						
TV shopping						

* Dollars shown in millions

Format 26 (Continued)

Customer Sales*

Last Three Years

19 ___

Product: _____

	Customer Type					
	Primary			Secondary		
	dollars	units	%	dollars	units	%
Retail:						
Discount store						
Department store						
Specialty store						
Variety store						
Supermarket						
Catalog showroom						
Convenience store						
Wholesale:						
Warehouse showroom						
Industrial distributor						
Special:						
Mail order						
Brokers						
Automatic/vending						
Door to door						
TV shopping						

* Dollars shown in millions

Format 26 (Continued)

Customer Sales*

Last Three Years

19 ___

Product: _____

	Customer Type					
	Primary			Secondary		
	dollars	units	%	dollars	units	%
Retail:						
Discount store						
Department store						
Specialty store						
Variety store						
Supermarket						
Catalog showroom						
Convenience store						
Wholesale:						
Warehouse showroom						
Industrial distributor						
Special:						
Mail order						
Brokers						
Automatic/vending						
Door to door						
TV shopping						

* Dollars shown in millions

Format 26 (Continued)

Customer Sales*

Next Three Years

19 ___

Product: _____

	Customer Type					
	Primary			Secondary		
	dollars	units	%	dollars	units	%
Retail:						
Discount store						
Department store						
Specialty store						
Variety store						
Supermarket						
Catalog showroom						
Convenience store						
Wholesale:						
Warehouse showroom						
Industrial distributor						
Special:						
Mail order						
Brokers						
Automatic/vending						
Door to door						
TV shopping						

* Dollars shown in millions

Format 26 (Continued)

Customer Sales*

Next Three Years

19 ___

Product: _____

	Customer Type					
	Primary			Secondary		
	dollars	units	%	dollars	units	%
Retail:						
Discount store						
Department store						
Specialty store						
Variety store						
Supermarket						
Catalog showroom						
Convenience store						
Wholesale:						
Warehouse showroom						
Industrial distributor						
Special:						
Mail order						
Brokers						
Automatic/vending						
Door to door						
TV shopping						

* Dollars shown in millions

Format 26 (Continued)

Customer Sales*

Next Three Years

19 ___

Product: _____

	Customer Type					
	Primary			Secondary		
	dollars	units	%	dollars	units	%
Retail:						
Discount store						
Department store						
Specialty store						
Variety store						
Supermarket						
Catalog showroom						
Convenience store						
Wholesale:						
Warehouse showroom						
Industrial distributor						
Special:						
Mail order						
Brokers						
Automatic/vending						
Door to door						
TV shopping						

* Dollars shown in millions

Format 27

Store-specific Performance (Origin/Point of Sale)

Product/Brand	Customer Type/Composite	Store Location

Format 28

Store-specific Location (Market/Trade Area)

	Defined Area		
Store/Location	Primary Block Level	Secondary Block Level	Tertiary Block Level

Format 29

Customer ID Data File

Customer Profile Type	Actual Customer

1. Customer variables	1. Customer:
	   a. Address:
	   b. Customer name:
	   c. Telephone number:

2. Customer variables	2. Customer:
	   a. Address:
	   b. Customer name:
	   c. Telephone number:

3. Customer variables	3. Customer:
	   a. Address:
	   b. Customer name:
	   c. Telephone number:

4. Customer variables	4. Customer:
	   a. Address:
	   b. Customer name:
	   c. Telephone number:

5. Customer variables	5. Customer:
	   a. Address:
	   b. Customer name:
	   c. Telephone number:

Analyzing Your Competition

Formats 30–42 should be used to help you analyze your competition.
See Unit 3 in Part 1 for explanations and examples of the formats.

Format 30

Competitor Identification

Competitor	Product Line			Target Market/Customers
	Past	Present	Future	

Format 31

Competition by Target Market

Last Three Years

19___

Competitor	Ranking	Market Share	Distribution

Format 31 (Continued)

Competition by Target Market

Last Three Years

19___

Competitor	Ranking	Market Share	Distribution

Format 31 (Continued)

Competition by Target Market

Next Three Years

19___

Competitor	Ranking	Market Share	Distribution

Format 31 (Continued)

Competition by Target Market

Next Three Years

19—

Competitor	Ranking	Market Share	Distribution

Format 31 (Continued)

Competition by Target Market

Next Three Years

19—

Competitor	Ranking	Market Share	Distribution

Format 31

Competition by Target Market

19___

Competitor	Ranking	Market Share	Distribution

Format 32

Competitor Sales Performance ($ thousands)

Last Three Years

	19 ___		19 ___		Rate of Growth	19 ___		Rate of Growth
	$	Units	$	Units	(%)	$	Units	(%)
Sales Potential:								
Overall:								
Product:								
Product:								
Product:								
Product:								
Product:								
Product:								
Product:								
Sales Forecast:								
Overall:								
Product:								
Product:								
Product:								
Product:								
Product:								
Product:								
Product:								

Competitor Sales Performance ($ thousands)

Last Three Years

	19 ___		19 ___		Rate of Growth	19 ___		Rate of Growth
	$	Units	$	Units	(%)	$	Units	(%)

Sales Potential:

Overall:

Product:

Product:

Product:

Product:

Product:

Product:

Product:

Sales Forecast:

Overall:

Product:

Product:

Product:

Product:

Product:

Product:

Product:

Format 33

Competitor Market Share ($ thousands)

Last Three Years

	19 ___	Units	19 ___	Units	Rate of Growth (%)	19 ___	Units	Rate of Growth (%)
Market Share (Relative to Market):								
Overall:								
Product:								
Product:								
Product:								
Product:								
Product:								
Product:								
Product:								
Market Share (Relative to Competition):								
Overall:								
Product:								
Product:								
Product:								
Product:								
Product:								
Product:								
Product:								

Format 33 (Continued)

Competitor Market Share ($ thousands)

Last Three Years

	19 ___	Units	19 ___	Units	Rate of Growth (%)	19 ___	Units	Rate of Growth (%)
Market Share (Relative to Market):								
Overall:								
Product:								
Product:								
Product:								
Product:								
Product:								
Product:								
Product:								
Market Share (Relative to Competition):								
Overall:								
Product:								
Product:								
Product:								
Product:								
Product:								
Product:								
Product:								

Format 34

Competitive Advantages of Competitors

Competitor	Strengths			
	A	B	C	D

A: Ability to satisfy customers' needs and desires
B: Track record and reputation
C: Staying power (financial resources)
D: Key personnel

Format 35

Competitive Disadvantages of Competitors

Competitor	Weaknesses			
	A	B	C	D

A: Ability to satisfy customers' needs and desires
B: Track record and reputation
C: Staying power (financial resources)
D: Key personnel

Format 36

Profitability and Financial Structure

Last Three Years

19 ___

Competitor: _____

Overall Product Line (Year Ending/Past):

Sales ($)

Sales (Units)

Rate of growth (%)

Cost of goods sold

Gross profit

Gross margin

Product (Year Ending/Future):

Sales ($)

Sales (Units)

Rate of growth (%)

Cost of goods sold

Gross profit

Gross margin

Format 36 (Continued)

Profitability and Financial Structure

Last Three Years

19 ___

Competitor: _____

Overall Product Line (Year Ending/Past):

Sales ($)

Sales (Units)

Rate of growth (%)

Cost of goods sold

Gross profit

Gross margin

Product (Year Ending/Future):

Sales ($)

Sales (Units)

Rate of growth (%)

Cost of goods sold

Gross profit

Gross margin

Format 36 (Continued)

Profitability and Financial Structure

Last Three Years

19 ___

Competitor: _____

Overall Product Line (Year Ending/Past):

Sales ($)

Sales (Units)

Rate of growth (%)

Cost of goods sold

Gross profit

Gross margin

Product (Year Ending/Future):

Sales ($)

Sales (Units)

Rate of growth (%)

Cost of goods sold

Gross profit

Gross margin

Format 36 (Continued)

Profitability and Financial Structure

Next Three Years

19 ___

Competitor: _____

Overall Product Line (Year Ending/Past):

Sales ($)

Sales (Units)

Rate of growth (%)

Cost of goods sold

Gross profit

Gross margin

Product (Year Ending/Future):

Sales ($)

Sales (Units)

Rate of growth (%)

Cost of goods sold

Gross profit

Gross margin

Format 36 (Continued)

Profitability and Financial Structure

Next Three Years

19 ___

Competitor: _____

Overall Product Line (Year Ending/Past):

Sales ($)

Sales (Units)

Rate of growth (%)

Cost of goods sold

Gross profit

Gross margin

Product (Year Ending/Future):

Sales ($)

Sales (Units)

Rate of growth (%)

Cost of goods sold

Gross profit

Gross margin

Format 36 (Continued)

Profitability and Financial Structure

Next Three Years

19 ___

Competitor: _____

Overall Product Line (Year Ending/Past):

Sales ($)

Sales (Units)

Rate of growth (%)

Cost of goods sold

Gross profit

Gross margin

Product (Year Ending/Future):

Sales ($)

Sales (Units)

Rate of growth (%)

Cost of goods sold

Gross profit

Gross margin

Format 37

Pricing/Cost Structure

Last Three Years

19 ___

Competitor: _____

Volume (Units)	Product			Product	
	1–5	6–10	11–15	1–5	5+
Price ($)					
Discount ($)					
Revenue ($)					
Costs ($)					
Gross profit ($)					
Price ($)					
Discount ($)					
Revenue ($)					
Costs ($)					
Gross profit ($)					
Price ($)					
Discount ($)					
Revenue ($)					
Costs ($)					
Gross profit ($)					

Format 37

Format 37 (Continued)

Pricing/Cost Structure

Last Three Years

19 ___

Competitor: _____

Volume (Units)	Product			Product	
	1–5	6–10	11–15	1–5	5+
Price ($)					
Discount ($)					
Revenue ($)					
Costs ($)					
Gross profit ($)					
Price ($)					
Discount ($)					
Revenue ($)					
Costs ($)					
Gross profit ($)					
Price ($)					
Discount ($)					
Revenue ($)					
Costs ($)					
Gross profit ($)					

Format 37 (Continued)

Pricing/Cost Structure

Last Three Years

19 ___

Competitor: _____

Volume (Units)	Product			Product	
	1–5	6–10	11–15	1–5	5+
Price ($)					
Discount ($)					
Revenue ($)					
Costs ($)					
Gross profit ($)					
Price ($)					
Discount ($)					
Revenue ($)					
Costs ($)					
Gross profit ($)					
Price ($)					
Discount ($)					
Revenue ($)					
Costs ($)					
Gross profit ($)					

Format 37 (Continued)

Pricing/Cost Structure

Next Three Years

19 ___

Competitor: _____

Volume (Units)	Product			Product	
	1–5	6–10	11–15	1–5	5+
Price ($)					
Discount ($)					
Revenue ($)					
Costs ($)					
Gross profit ($)					
Price ($)					
Discount ($)					
Revenue ($)					
Costs ($)					
Gross profit ($)					
Price ($)					
Discount ($)					
Revenue ($)					
Costs ($)					
Gross profit ($)					

Pricing/Cost Structure

Next Three Years

19 ___

Competitor: _____

Volume (Units)	Product			Product	
	1–5	6–10	11–15	1–5	5+
Price ($)					
Discount ($)					
Revenue ($)					
Costs ($)					
Gross profit ($)					
Price ($)					
Discount ($)					
Revenue ($)					
Costs ($)					
Gross profit ($)					
Price ($)					
Discount ($)					
Revenue ($)					
Costs ($)					
Gross profit ($)					

Format 37 (Continued)

Pricing/Cost Structure

Next Three Years

19 ___

Competitor: _____

Volume (Units)	Product			Product	
	1–5	**6–10**	**11–15**	**1–5**	**5+**
Price ($)					
Discount ($)					
Revenue ($)					
Costs ($)					
Gross profit ($)					
Price ($)					
Discount ($)					
Revenue ($)					
Costs ($)					
Gross profit ($)					
Price ($)					
Discount ($)					
Revenue ($)					
Costs ($)					
Gross profit ($)					

Format 38

Marketing Expenses by Competitor

Last Three Years

Marketing Function	19 ___ ($)	Percentage of Total Sales	19 ___ ($)	Percentage of Total Sales	19 ___ ($)	Percentage of Total Sales
Marketing research						
Product/new product development						
Pricing						
Distribution						
Sales						
Advertising						
Promotions						
Public relations						
Legal						
Total						
Percentage of sales						

Format 38 (Continued)

Marketing Expenses by Competitor

Next Three Years

Marketing Function	19 ___ ($)	Percentage of Total Sales	19 ___ ($)	Percentage of Total Sales	19 ___ ($)	Percentage of Total Sales
Marketing research						
Product/new product development						
Pricing						
Distribution						
Sales						
Advertising						
Promotions						
Public relations						
Legal						
Total						
Percentage of sales						

Format 39

Media Usage Expenses by Competitor

Last Three Years	19 ___ ($)	Percent of Total Advertising Budget	19 ___ ($)	Percent of Total Advertising Budget	19 ___ ($)	Total
Direct response:						
Mail						
Phone						
Cable TV						
Interactive TV						
Video						
Fax						
Computer						
Outdoor response:						
Billboard						
General signage						
Transit						
Television viewership:						
Cable						
Broadcast						
Home shopping						
Infomercials						
Radio listenership:						
Spot						
Print readership:						
Newspaper						
Magazine						
Insert (FSI)						
Yellow Pages						
Special viewership:						
Sports						
POP						
Floor displays						
Coupons						
Sales premiums						
Total						

Format 39 (Continued)

Media Usage Expenses by Competitor

Next Three Years	19 __ ($)	Percent of Total Advertising Budget	19 __ ($)	Percent of Total Advertising Budget	19 __ ($)	Total
Direct response:						
Mail						
Phone						
Cable TV						
Interactive TV						
Video						
Fax						
Computer						
Outdoor response:						
Billboard						
General signage						
Transit						
Television viewership:						
Cable						
Broadcast						
Home shopping						
Infomercials						
Radio listenership:						
Spot						
Print readership:						
Newspaper						
Magazine						
Insert (FSI)						
Yellow Pages						
Special viewership:						
Sports						
POP						
Floor displays						
Coupons						
Sales premiums						
Total						

Format 40

Research and Development Activities

Next Three Years

19 __

Competitor	Stage	Release Date	Impact

A: Direct, indirect
B: Suppliers/distributors
C: Customers

Format 40 (Continued)

Research and Development Activities

Next Three Years

19 ___

Competitor	A.	B.	C.

A: Direct, indirect
B: Suppliers/distributors
C: Customers

Format 40 (Continued)

Research and Development Activities

Next Three Years

19 ___

Competitor	A.	B.	C.

A: Direct, indirect
B: Suppliers/distributors
C: Customers

Format 41

Opportunity Projections

Next Three Years

19 ___

New Competitors	Products	Estimated Base Price	Features/Benefits

Format 41

Format 41 (Continued)

Opportunity Projections

Next Three Years

19 ___

New Competitors   **Products**   **Estimated Base Price**   **Features/Benefits**

Format 41 (Continued)

Opportunity Projections

Next Three Years

19 ____

New Competitors	Products	Estimated Base Price	Features/Benefits

Format 42

Competitors' Barriers to Entry

Competitor	A. Time	B. Technology	C. Key Personnel	D. Customer Limitations	E. Existing Patents and Trademarks

Working within Regulatory Restrictions

Formats 43–45 should be used to help you work within regulatory restrictions. See Unit 4 in Part 1 for explanations and examples of the formats.

Format 43

Laws/Rules/Regulations

Product	Past	Current	Future	Agency/Legislative Control

Format 44

Anticipated Market Changes

Product	Factor Type	Effect on Market

Format 45

Cost of Meeting Market Requirements

Product	Restriction	Timing	Cost to Comply

Comparing Your Market Analysis with Existing Market Research

Format 46 should be used to help you compare your market analysis with existing market research. See Unit 5 in Part 1 for explanations and examples of the formats.

Format 46

Degree of Marketplace Demand

Product	Previous Marketing Studies	Date	Findings	Adjustments (if any)

About the Author

David Parmerlee is a marketing analyst and planner who works with selected clients. He is past Vice President of the Marketing Management Services Group at American Marketmetrics, Inc. A marketer with more than 12 years of experience, his approach has a financial orientation rather than the more traditional communications approach. His background is in secondary and audit research with a focus on process-based planning and implementation.

Parmerlee has worked for several major corporations, including Anheuser-Busch, Pitney Bowes, and Arthur Young (now Ernst & Young). He has represented clients in industrial, consumer, and service-based markets and has written articles for regional and national publications. He is a member of the Direct Marketing Association and the American Mar-keting Association, where he serves on the board of directors and the national board of standards for professional development and certification.

Parmerlee received his degrees in marketing and advertising from Ball State University in Muncie, Indiana. He is also certified as a consultant specializing in training and ethics.

⋏⋏ AMERICAN **MARKETING** ASSOCIATION

YOU NEVER GET ENOUGH . . .

As a marketing professional you'll never get enough information about marketing. The body of knowledge is being added to constantly. Success stories, and even stories of failure, are written daily.

There's only one way to stay up-to-date with the latest academic theories, the "war" stories, the global techniques, and the leading technologies.

Become a member of the American Marketing Association.

For a free membership information kit,
call us at 312-648-0536
FAX us at 312-993-7542
write us at 250 S. Wacker Drive, Chicago, Illinois 60606
or contact your local AMA chapter.

AM AMERICAN MARKETING ASSOCIATION

AMA MARKETING TOOLBOX

A Series of Informative Guides to the Strategies and Practical Skills That Build Successful Marketing Programs

The **AMA Marketing Toolbox** is a unique source of information, ideas, and direction for anyone building an effective marketing program or improving current marketing activities. Each book in this series covers a key marketing function. Whether you are expanding your customer base, exploring new markets, or launching a new product or service, these easy-to-use books provide countless ideas that will help you save time, make the best possible use of your resources, and find creative solutions to marketing problems.

Developed with the American Marketing Association, the **AMA Marketing Toolbox** guides you through every critical marketing task and provides the tools—model formats, checklists, and boilerplate documents—to implement those tasks quickly, accurately, and effectively.

Identifying the Right Markets

This book will help you perform a complete and thorough market analysis for your company, product, or service. By working through the marketing tasks and processes in Part 1, you'll:

- Define how each market you target is structured and measure your position within it

- Profile your best customers and prospects and discover *how* and *why* they buy

- Analyze your competitors and review *their* marketing

- Evaluate your marketing and make adjustments that respond to market forces

Part 2 equips you with more than 40 formats that, once completed, will provide an accurate base of information from which to make intelligent marketing decisions.

AMA Marketing Toolbox includes:

Identifying the Right Markets
Selecting the Right Products and Services
Evaluating Marketing Strengths and Weaknesses
Developing Successful Marketing Strategies
Preparing the Marketing Plan

US $24.95 / CAN $34.95

ISBN 0-8442-3576-8

9 780844 235769   52495

AMERICAN MARKETING ASSOCIATION

NTC Business Books
NTC/Contemporary Publishing Company